The Origin and Development of Dougong and Zaojing in Early China

Jing Xie

ANTHEM PRESS

Anthem Press
An imprint of Wimbledon Publishing Company
www.anthempress.com

This edition first published in UK and USA 2023
by ANTHEM PRESS
75–76 Blackfriars Road, London SE1 8HA, UK
or PO Box 9779, London SW19 7ZG, UK
and
244 Madison Ave #116, New York, NY 10016, USA

British Library Cataloguing-in-Publication Data
A catalogue record for this book is available from the British Library.

Library of Congress Cataloging-in-Publication Data
A catalog record for this book has been requested.
2022950518

ISBN-13: 978-1-78527-942-3 (Pbk)
ISBN-10: 1-78527-942-4 (Pbk)

Cover Credit: Photographer Ye Wei, photo courtesy of Baoguosi Museum of Ancient Architecture, Ningbo.

This title is also available as an e-book.

To my father Xie Hongchuan 谢洪川

CONTENTS

ACKNOWLEDGMENTS

Early Chinese cities are well acknowledged for their cosmic-inspired development pattern. This practice is probably more consistently apparent than in other countries. Yet early Chinese temples seemed to have failed in their architecture, if the intent was to hold a dialogue with the gods, as the churches in the West did. Is the early Chinese architecture, particularly the great halls for palaces and temples, too feeble to celebrate soaring human spirits? Before answering this question, I would like to provide a brief backdrop of meaningful earth–heaven dialogues that evidently were captured by literature and architecture from the Early West period.

In classical antiquity, Plato documented the conversation between Socrates and Glaucon regarding the explanation of the "good." "Which of the gods in heaven was the lord of this element [i.e. the good]? Whose is that light which makes the eye see perfectly and the visible to appear?" asked Socrates. "You mean the sun, as you and all mankind say." answered Glaucon without hesitation. Their conversation continued. The key point illustrated by Plato is that the sun illuminates things by its light, thus objects and beauty can be fully visible to the eye. Socrates called the sun, "the child of the good," for the good has a much higher place of honor than the sun, and illuminates the soul with intelligence to perceive and understand knowledge and truth (*The Republic*, Book VI, 238–246).

The Greek philosophers influenced the Ancient Romans, among them being the wise emperor Marcus Aurelius, who believed that the stars, like the sun, would sublimate human souls, as he stated in *Meditations* (Book 7, 64): "Watch the stars in their courses as though you were accompanying them on their way, and reflect perpetually on how the elements are constantly changing from one to another; for the thought of these things purifies us from the defilement of our earthly existence."

Elevated morality seems to have had an inherent link with the empyrean. This line of thought, if not echoed intellectually in text, materialized through architecture in the Middle Ages. Churches emerged and became widespread in Europe with their splendid interiors reflecting human imagination about the heavens. Indeed through the churches, the notion of heaven as the destiny for the deceased good was strongly imprinted in medieval Christian minds. In a sense, the beliefs about "good" would build up a moral edifice that could also be transformed into a material edifice, the two being mutually enhancing.

With envy and admiration toward the intellectual and architectural discourses of the heavens in the West, I shall return to the question imposed at the beginning. Compared to the temples and churches in the West, the Chinese religious structures are indeed inferior in their scale and architectural vocabulary for expressing grandness and vertical connection to the heavens. Such ineloquence was also present in the Chinese language: in particular, there is no other pair of words like "good" and "god" which are so closely connected in moral philosophy and which have invoked so much intellectual exploration. However, the answer, as the book has found, is quite the opposite. This perhaps verifies Prof. Yi-Fu Tuan's assertion that outstanding intellectual and artistic achievements transcend time and place (*Dear Colleague*, 46).

Two chapters, Chapters 2 and 3, have come out of my published papers. The first is "Pillar of Heaven: The Symbolic Function of Column-and-Bracket Sets in the Han Dynasty," *Architectural History*, vol. 63 (2020). The second is "From Earth to Heaven: The Origin and Development of Zaojing in Early China," *arq: Architectural Research Quarterly*, vol. 23 (2019). I would like to thank Cambridge University Press for permission to reuse these two papers, and also my thanks to two editors, Dr. Anthony Gerbino and Dr. Juliet Odgers, for their assistance in the journal publication process respectively. The book benefited from the constructive comments from six anonymous reviewers in its proposal stage and three anonymous reviewers in the final submission. Prof. Ronald Knapp has kindly offered his help in proofreading the whole manuscript and providing valuable comments. I am highly indebted to his unfailing support.

I would like to dedicate this book to my father, a truly good person who recently departed from us. Like the sun, he did and will unceasingly illuminate my world.

PROLOGUE

Dougong 斗栱 and *zaojing* 藻井 are two important architectural elements that were constructed in the great halls of China's royal palaces, major temples, as well as in the underground tombs of social elites. The former consists of *dou* (block) and *gong* (arm) that form a structural unit as bracket set. Often in multiple forms known as *chonggong* 重栱 and placed on the top of columns and beams, *dougong* plays a critical role in holding the upper structure securely (Figure 1). The latter is a special structure sunken into the ceiling, often profusely decorated with carvings and colorful paintings in various motifs (Figures 2–4). *Zaojing* is translated variously as "caisson," "cupola," and "lantern ceiling."[1]

The construction of *zaojing*, quite often, would involve *dougong* as either structural units or decorative elements. Both of them would appear at the upper proportion of architecture, and they were once the symbols of social status in imperial China. Sumptuary law in the Tang dynasty (618–907), for example, codified that nobles below the royal family members could not adopt the construction treatment of *zaojing* and *chonggong* (i.e., *dougong* in its multiple form) in their houses.[2] Although housing control was loosened in the Song dynasty (960–1279), *zaojing* and *chonggong* were still prestigious architectural features that were forbidden in commoners' houses. In addition, their houses were not allowed to adopt the five-color decoration motif.[3] In the Ming dynasty (1368–1644), sumptuary law for housing seemed to be tightened up, as it stipulated that the court officials' houses could neither build the double-eave roof and *chonggong* nor the painted *zaojing*. The commoner's houses could not apply *dougong* or colored paintings.[4]

The seamless connection between *zaojing* and *dougong* is also reflected in the famous Song construction manual *Yingzao fashi* 营造法式 (1103), in which

1 Nancy S. Steinhardt, *Chinese Architecture in an Age of Turmoil, 200–600* (Honolulu, 2014), 271.
2 Wang Pu, *Tang huiyao* (Beijing, 1955), ch. 31, 575.
3 Tuotuo et al., *Songshi* (Beijing, 1977), ch. 154, 3600.
4 Zhang Tingyu, *Mingshi* (Beijing, 2014), vol. 2, ch. 68, 699.

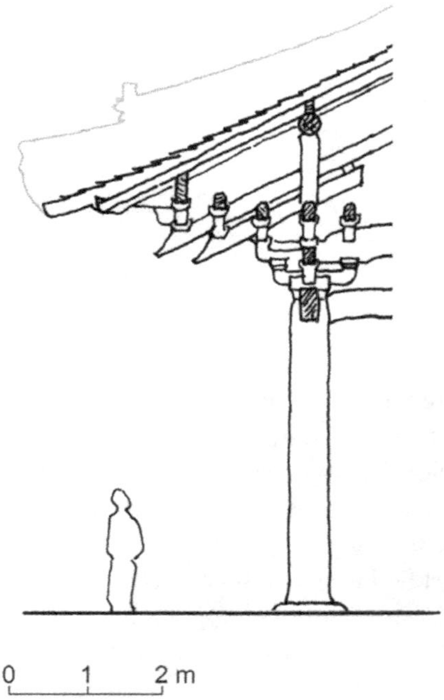

Figure 1 A segmented structural section, including the pedestal, column, bracket sets, purlin, and up to the roof rafters (author's drawing, 2020).

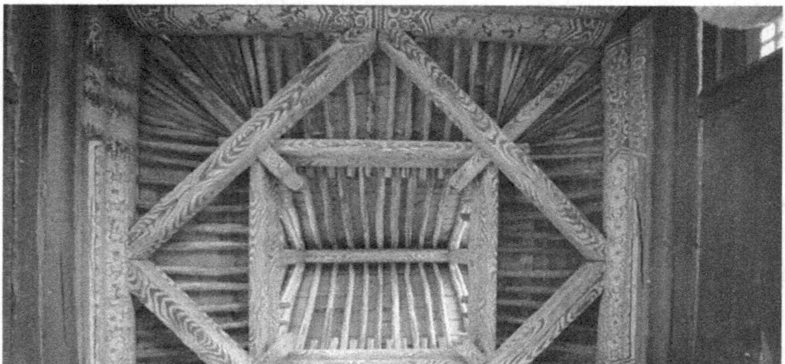

Figure 2 *Zaojing* in a pavilion of the Hanging Temple 悬空寺, built into a cliff near Mount Heng in Hunyuan County, Datong, Shanxi Province, originally in the late Northern Wei dynasty (386–534) (Photo by Fu Ruixue, 2015).

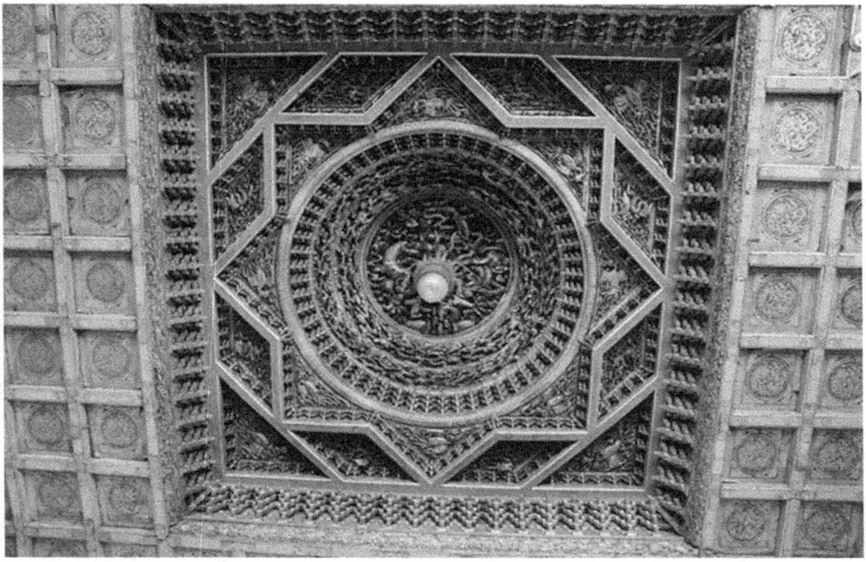

Figure 3 *Zaojing* in the Hall of Mental Cultivation 养心殿 in the Forbidden City, which was built in 1537 and rebuilt between 1723 and 1735, Beijing (Photo by Fu Ruixue, 2014).

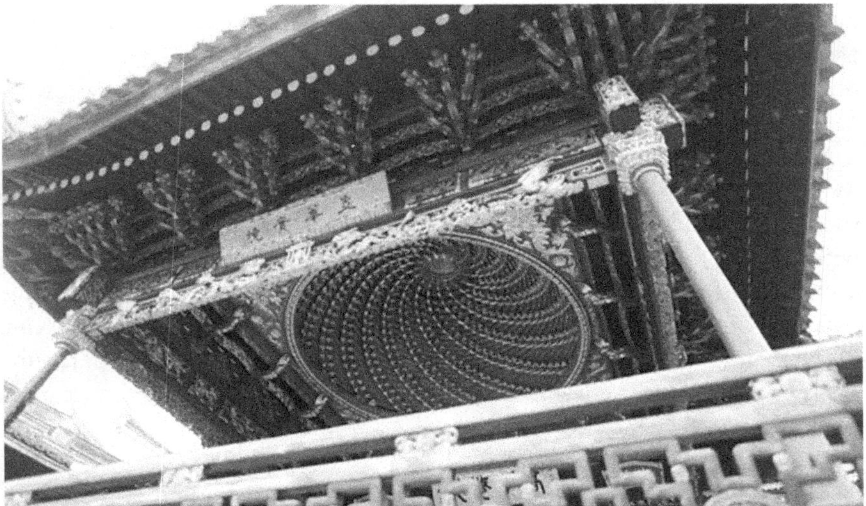

Figure 4 *Zaojing* in the theatre pavilion of the Qin's Ancestral Temple 秦氏支祠, Ningbo, Zhejiang Province, built between 1923 and 1925 (author's photo, 2016).

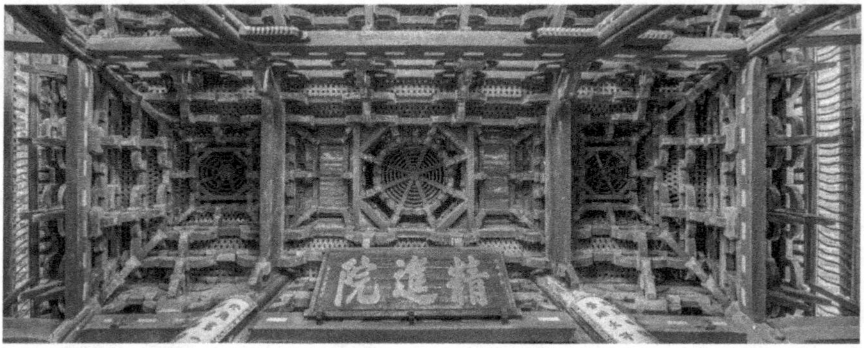

Figure 5 *Dougong* and *zaojing* in the great hall of Baoguo Temple, Ningbo, Zhejiang Province (photo by Ye Wei, Baoguosi Museum of Ancient Architecture).

zaojing has a particular term *douba zaojing* 斗八藻井, suggesting a dome-like *zaojing* supported by eight *dougong* units.[5] This literary account is perfectly manifested by a relic of *zaojing* built in 1013 that remains in the great hall of Baoguo Temple, in Ningbo, Zhejiang Province (Figure 5).

As unique and important elements in classical Chinese architecture, *dougong* and *zaojing* have been richly studied by scholars from the West and Asia ever since the early twentieth century. Particularly the discourse on *dougong* has appeared as an essential component in the studies of traditional Chinese architecture. Le Jiazao probably was the first scholar who investigated *dougong* as a research topic and systematically surveyed the various terminologies describing *dougong* in the Chinese literature.[6] With a critical view toward Le's published book in 1933, Liang Sicheng and his team started to examine historic buildings in general and *dougong* in particular through the Society for the Study of Chinese Architecture (established in 1930).[7] As the key member of the Society too, Liu Dunzhen and his team also studied Chinese architecture with a focus on literature studies. Their works influenced a long line of architectural historians who joined the Society as assistants at the beginning, such as Chen Mingda, Luo Zhewen, Fu Xinian, and Yang Hongxun. Yet the most studies on *dougong* remain typological due to its structural nature. Pan Dehua, for example, one of Luo Zhewen's disciples, with more than

5 Li Jie, *Yingzao fashi* (Beijing, 2011), 61.

6 Le Jiazao, *Zhongguo jianzhu shi* (Nanchang, 2018), 71–79.

7 Liang Sicheng's critical view was originally published in 1934 in the article, "Du Le Jiazao *Zhongguo jianhzu shi* pimiu," in: Liang Sicheng, *Zhongguo jianhzu shi* (Tianjin, 1998), 361–370.

40 years experience on Chinese architecture research and practice, spent 12 years on writing the book *dougong* (2011) that includes hundreds of drawings and photos of *dougong* from different period and region.[8] It is a meticulous historic documentation of *dougong*.

English scholarship on *dougong* is largely evident in a number of publications by Alexandra Harrer, in particular her PhD dissertation based on the extensive field research of fan-shaped bracket sets in Shanxi Province and literature study on Chinese architecture and history.[9] There was a breakthrough in Jiren Feng's research *Chinese Architecture and Metaphor* (2012). From an architectural humanities perspective, Feng inquires about the symbolic meanings of column and *dougong* in the Song dynasty. Recent studies on *dougong* seem to be more diverse: some analyze *dougong* in a parametric design purview and others explore wider applications of its tectonic trait.

Compared to *dougong*, *zaojing* is a less studied topic. Liang Sicheng and Liu Zhiping briefly discussed *zaojing* in 1937, in a similar vein as their collective publication on *dougong*.[10] A few years later, Alexander Soper published his classical paper "The 'Dome of Heaven' in Asia," in which *zaojing* was contextualized in a process of transmission from the West to the East.[11] Soper's paper was critically reviewed by Nancy S. Steinhardt in her study of Chinese architecture between 200 and 600.[12] In the section of the ceilings, her study of *zaojing* not only connects to domes of heaven in the Western context but also connects to her early research on octagonal ceilings in China.[13] Most Chinese scholarship on *zaojing* is related to the remaining *zaojing* from Mogao Caves in Dunhuang, Gansu Province.[14] The documentation of the *zaojing* is evident in a number of published photo albums and collections of drawings.[15] Digitalization of Mogao Caves is also online now.[16] Accordingly,

8 Pan Dehua and Pan Yexiang, *Dougong* (Nanjing, 2011), 2 vols.

9 Alexandra Harrer, *Fan-Shaped Bracket Sets and Their Application in Religious Timber Architecture of Shanxi Province* (University of Pennsylvania, 2010).

10 Liang Sicheng and Liu Zhiping, "Zaojing tianhua jianshuo," in: *Liang Sicheng quanji* (Beijing, 2001), VI, 416–421; Liang Sicheng and Liu Zhiping, "Dougong jianshuo," in: Ibid, 291–324.

11 Alexander Coburn Soper, "The 'Dome of Heaven' in Asia," *The Art Bulletin*, vol. 29, 4 (1947):225–248.

12 Steinhardt, *Chinese Architecture in an Age of Turmoil*, 270–283.

13 Nancy S. Steinhardt, "Octagonal Halls and Octagonal Ceilings," Proceedings from the Second International Conference on Chinese Architectural History, Hangzhou, August 2001, 282–289.

14 For example, Xiao Mo, *Dunhuang jianzhu yanjiu* (Beijing, 2019), 385–394.

15 For example, The Editorial Committee of the complete murals in Dunhuang, ed., *Zhongguo Dunhuang bihua quanji* (Tianjin, 2002), vol. 1–11.

16 Please see Digital Dunhuang official website: https://www.e-dunhuang.com/.

patterns, decoration motifs, and symbolisms of the *zaojing* from different historic periods in Mogao Caves have been studied. In English scholarship, a more comprehensive study of *zaojing* is evident by Jun Hu's PhD dissertation, in which the early Chinese literature associated with *zaojing* has been extensively discussed.[17]

Apart from research, architectural practice in modern times is also drawing inspiration from historical structures, particularly in the wide context of heritage conservation. In relation to *dougong*, it is also an iconic element of traditional architecture in Japan, Korea, and Southeast Asian countries influenced by China. Tadao Ando, for example, reinterpreted the wooden columns and bracket sets as a major feature in his design for the Japan Pavilion at the Universal Exposition in Seville in 1992. The China Pavilion at Expo 2010 in Shanghai, designed by He Jingtang and his team as the exhibition's largest and tallest structure, is another instance. Colloquially known as the "oriental crown," the China Pavilion inspired a nickname clearly derived from its mammoth *dougong* system, supported by four giant pillars. Although there is not a prominent case for adaptive or creative reuse of *zaojing* by celebrity architects so far, *zaojing* widely appears in numerous public buildings such as The Great Hall of the People in Beijing and many museums throughout China.

From the above brief review of the scholarship and heritage practice concerning *dougong* and *zaojing*, the importance of these two elements is patent and they seem to be a defining identity of Chinese traditional architecture. For most scholarship concentrates on the surviving structures from the Tang dynasty and afterward, questions remain as to how *dougong* and *zaojing* come into being in the first place? What was their symbolic function other than being a structural or decorative form in early China, particularly before the Song dynasty that has been investigated by Feng? Has the heritage practice in modern times truly grasped the essence of these two important architectural elements?

This book thus inquiries about the origin and development of *dougong* and *zaojing* in the Han period and prior, deciphering the embedded cultural meanings. In structuring the book contents, much weight has been given to *dougong*. This is because not only historic evidence and scholarship of *dougong* are overwhelmingly abundant than that of *zaojing*, but also *dougong* as a structure unit often contributed to the fabrication of *zaojing* (see Figures 3 and 5).

---

17 Jun Hu, *Embracing the Circle: Domical Buildings in East Asian Architecture ca. 200–750* (Princeton University, 2014), 17–19.

As far as we know, the term *dougong* first appeared in a Buddhist text of 616, and the earliest surviving wooden buildings with *dougong* can be only traced back to the Tang dynasty.[18] Yet there are different terms from the earlier literature describing the Chinese bracket set system (i.e., *dougong*). Similarly, the term *zaojing* and its textual variations widely appeared in the early literature, mostly from the Han dynasty (206 BCE–220 CE). During the Han period, forms of *dougong* and *zaojing* were also manifest in numerous tomb structures, reliefs, pottery models of buildings (*mingqi*, 明器), murals, freestanding stone pillars (*que*, 阙), and even utensils.

More interestingly, all these architectural, pictorial, and literary elements of *dougong* and *zaojing* from the Han period are centralized on representing one particular theme, that is, as this book will argue, a longing for heaven. This human struggle of connecting to heaven also had its precedents in the Chinese Bronze Age (c. 2000–500 BCE). Evidence of a close relationship between architecture and bronze vessels from the Shang and Zhou dynasties (c. 1600–256 BCE) is also traceable. This relationship is articulated through analyzing the archeological findings, such as bronze vessels, bronze furniture, bronze components in architecture, and excavated building foundations, and relevant literature.

Driven by the religious struggles for heavens in early China, architectural elements *dougong* and *zaojing* were created with amazing imaginations other than technical and functional considerations since they effectively sustained a human dialogue with the heavens. Compared to their later technically oriented development from the Tang to the Qing dynasties (c. 618–1912), and their modern preservation and innovative reinterpretation, this book contends that the rich cultural meanings formerly embodied in *dougong* and *zaojing* have almost disappeared. Considering the transcendental quality that *dougong* and *zaojing* had particularly in the Han dynasty in compellingly expressing a mystical and magical world-view, this subsequently resulted in a tangible loss of China's architectural heritage.

18 For the earliest use of the term *dougong*, see Zhong Xiaoqing, 'Dougong, puzuo, yu puzuo ceng', *Zhongguo jianzhu shilun huikan*, 1 (2008), 4. (All Chinese terms have been rendered in the standard *hanyu pinyin* system of romanisation and have been italicised in accordance with scholarly convention. I have used simplified Chinese characters and followed Chinese surname order, unless they are habitually rendered otherwise in previous publications.)

Chapter 1

SEARCHING FOR THE ORIGIN OF *DOUGONG* IN THE CHINESE BRONZE AGE

Among various research topics on *dougong*, the most intriguing question is how *dougong* was formed in the first place. There have been seemingly ceaseless efforts in searching for the origin of *dougong*. Yang Hongxun, for example, pointed out that the birth of *dougong* was a result of structural evolution. In early wooden architecture, he posits that there was a physical transformation of posts supporting an eave to an oblique beam, then to a curved beam, and eventually to a curved arm with block (Figure 1.1).[1] In the essay titled "The Origin and Development of *Dougong*," Han Baode ponders over the early forms of *dougong*. Through inquiring about the physical remains and literature related to *dougong*, mainly from the Han dynasty, he challenges one theory that *dougong* was derived from the stone architecture in the West. Han raises the hypothesis that the birth and development of *dougong* was most likely influenced by religious forces.[2] Guo Huayu also enquires about the origin and development of *dougong* and from a typological perspective, presents some early cases reflecting the forms of *dougong* in chronological order, including a bronze vessel, a lacquerware illustration, a bronze table, some pottery models, and their associations with many remaining historic buildings.[3]

According to archaeological discoveries, Chinese architecture can be well traced back to the Neolithic settlements. Many foundations of palace and religious buildings from the Chinese Bronze Age have also been excavated. Yet the form of *dougong* is largely absent from these archaeological sites. It is in the Han dynasty that the flourishing of *dougong* is widely evident (as discussed in Chapter 2). Certainly, there is a gap between the absence and the flourishing of *dougong*, which suggests a long formative period of centuries of *dougong* prior to the Han period.

---

1 Yang Hongxun, "Dougong qiyuan kaocha," in: *Jianzhu kaoguxue lunwenji* (Beijing, 1987), 253–267.

2 Han Baode, *Ming-Qing jianzhu er'lun/dougong de qiyuan yu fazhan* (Beijing, 2014), 83–189.

3 Guo Huayu, *Zhongguo gudian jianzhu xingzhi yuanliu* (Wuhan, 2015), 223–238.

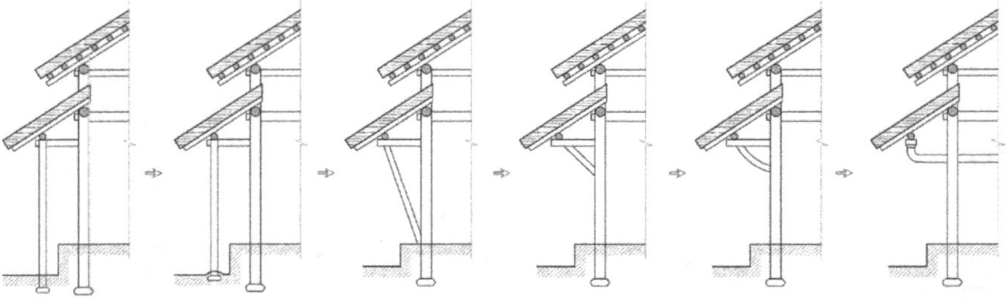

Figure 1.1 Diagrams showing transformation from the eave post to the bracket arm (author's drawing, based on Yang, *Jianzhu kaoguxue lunwenji*, 259, fig. 8).

In examining the early form of *dougong*, some research has observed the emergence of *dougong* patterns in the bronze vessels and furniture from the Shang and Zhou dynasties. Yet these studies only briefly discuss the physical form and its association with the bracket set system in much later architecture. Chapter 1 thus revisits the topics on the origin of *dougong*. Through examining a number of bronze vessels, bronze furniture, and bronze structural components from early China that relate to *dougong* in particular and architecture in general, the research attempts to articulate a possible path of the development of the *dougong* bracket set during the Chinese Bronze Age.

Bronze Utensils and Culture

Almost all the bronze utensils unearthed so far possess a noticeable characteristic. Throughout the Bronze Age in China, about 1,500 years, most bronze utensils were not produced for production tools such as agricultural implements. Rather, they were mainly ritual utensils in diverse forms and played a critical role in religious, political, and spiritual spheres of the society. Even the bronze weapons and chariots were likely used more frequently on parade than in the battlefield.[4]

Prior to the Qin dynasty (221–206 BCE), bronze utensils were always possessed only by kings and the aristocracy, and their presence was confined to the palace buildings and great temples. The right of manufacturing and

4 This is rather a synthesized view from the following scholarship, Zhang Xin, "Qingtong qi liyi lunyao," *Kaogu yanjiu*, 2006(00):573; K. C. Chang, *Art, Myth, and Ritual: The Path to Political Authority in Ancient China* (Cambridge, 1983), 108; Herrlee Glessner Creel, *The Birth of China: A Survey of the Formative Period of Chinese Civilization* (London, 1936), 119; Wu Hung, *Monumentality in Early Chinese Art and Architecture* (Stanford, 1995), 63–76.

possessing ritual bronze utensils was considered as a mandate of heaven. Political power was to a great extent legitimated by the ownership of ritual bronze utensils. Referring to three key aspects of bronze utensil, that is, material, manufacture, and function, Zhang Xin expounds why the Chinese ancients selected bronze utensils for sacrificial vessels and also as an important medium for communication between human beings and divinities.[5] It was chiefly because bronze utensils not only required a rigid and laborious process to make but also embodied the highest achievements in technology and craftsmanship at that time. In that sense, they were more suitable than other artifacts to serve both religious and political rites.

Not only diverse in their types and forms, bronze utensils are also full of symbols with decorative motifs, including different animals and human/divine figures, prevailing. Much research has been dedicated to the iconography of Chinese pictorial bronze utensils from the Shang and Zhou dynasties.[6] Regarding the initial purpose of casting bronze utensils, perhaps no scholar could avoid quoting the classical text from *Zuozhuan* 左传 (*The Commentary of Zuo*, covering a period from 722 to 468 BCE). The text recorded a conversation between the King of Chu and Wangsun Man in 606 BCE, concerning the utility of *ding* 鼎, the most prestigious form of bronze vessel.

> The *ding* were cast to represent *wu* 物. All the *wu* were represented, and [instructions were given] for the preparations to be made in reference to them, so that the people might know the helping and the harming spirits. Thus the people would avoid meeting with the injurious things when they went among the rivers, marshes, hills, and forests; and the hill-spirits, monstrous things, and water-sprites would not meet with them [to do them injury]. Hereby a harmony was secured between heaven and earth, and all enjoyed the blessings of heaven.[7]

The very word *wu*, to K. C. Chang, meant "animals with power" or "animal offerings."[8] Yet from the quoted text above, it also refers to mythical creatures

5 Zhang, "Qingtong qi liyi lunyao," 573.

6 For example, see Charles D. Weber, "Chinese Pictorial Bronze Vessels of the Late Chou Period, Parts I–IV," *Artibus Asiae*, 1966, vol. 28(2/3):107–154; 1966, vol. 28(4):271–311; 1967, vol. 29(2/3):115–192; 1968, vol. 30(2/3):145–236; Elizabeth Childs-Johnson, "Urban daemons of early Shang," *Archaeological Research in Asia*, June 2018, vol. 14, 135–150; Xie Qinguo and Zhang Dan, "Guanxiang zhiqi; Xia Shang shiqi qingtongqi tuxiang de wenhua fuhao biaozheng," *Signs & Media*, 2018(02):80.

7 Zuo Qiouming, *Zuozhuan zhushu*, ch. 21, 433–434. The English translation is based on Chang, *Art, Myth, and Ritual*, 63–64, slightly modified by the author.

8 Chang, *Art, Myth, and Ritual*, 64–65.

such as spirits, monsters, and sprites. Such pictorial representation of natural and supernatural elements can be readily linked to the later decorative motifs in traditional China architecture. In a similar way, premodern architecture was also striving to establish a harmonious connection between heaven and earth through its exuberant decor. Demonstrated by extensive scholarship, bronze utensils have united the arts, religions, politics, and historiography in one physical medium. Considering the mutual connection between bronze utensils and architecture—both a physical embodiment of the culture and required certain techniques in their making—it is hard to deny that *dougong* in architecture and that in bronze vessel/furniture would share some common traits.

The Bronze Vessel and Architecture

The bronze vessels from early China not only served ritual ceremony but also had a close relationship with contemporaneous architecture. In the making of some bronze vessels, local architecture possibly was taken as a reference point. This is particularly true in the case of a bronze vessel from the Fuhao (Lady Hao) tomb unearthed in Anyang, Henan Province. This bronze vessel is named *oufangyi* 偶方彝 (Figure 1.2). According to the archaeological finding, the Fuhao tomb was located in the archaeological

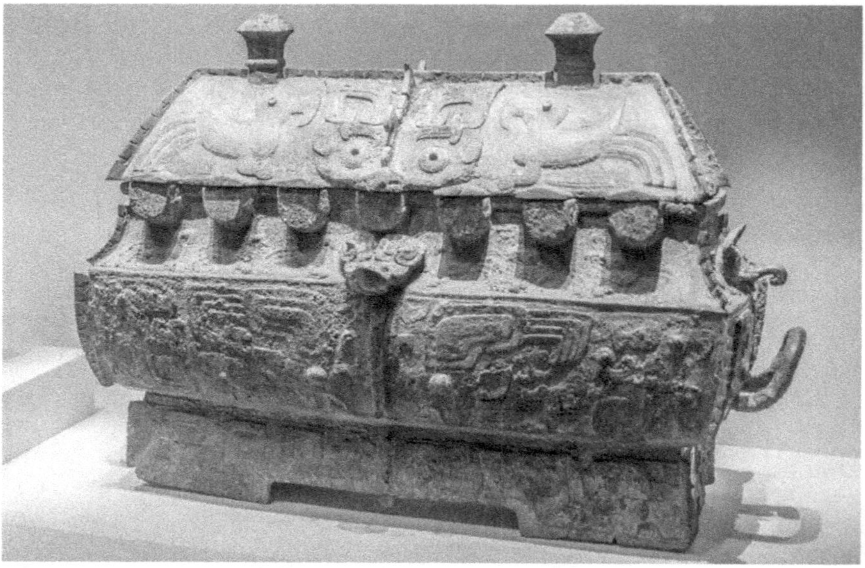

Figure 1.2 The Lady Hao's *oufangyi* from the Shang dynasty (National Museum, Beijing, photo by Fu Ruixue, 2013).

remains of Yinxu, a capital city in the Late Shang period (c. 1300–1046 BCE). In the bottom of the vessel, two words "Fu Hao 妇好" are engraved, indicating that its owner, Lady Hao, was the wife of the Shang king Wu Ding 武丁 (?–1192 BCE).

Fangyi 方彝 is a special wine container from the late Shang and Zhou dynasties (c. 1300–256 BCE) (Figure 1.3). *Fang* 方 means square, reflecting the square form of this type of utensil. Considering the size of the Fuhao *fangyi*: length 88.2 cm, width 17.5 cm, and height 60 cm, it is like two *fangyi* join together as one. Thus, the name *oufangyi*, meaning twin *fangyi*, was coined.

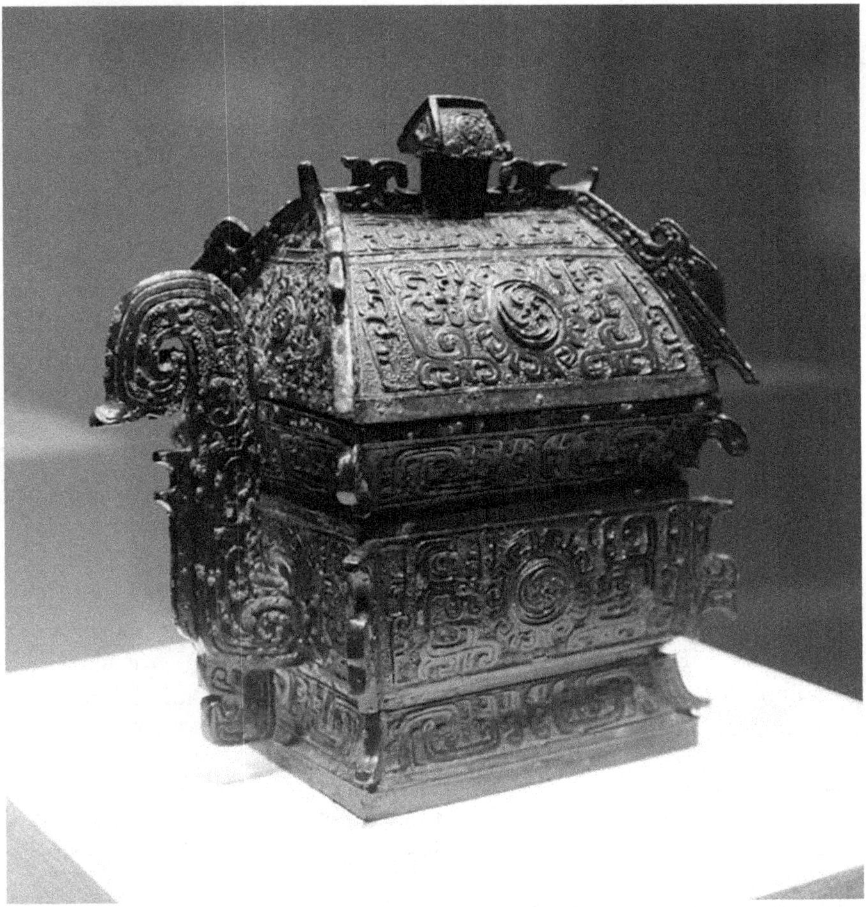

Figure 1.3 A *fangyi* from the Zhou dynasty (National Museum, Beijing, author's photo, 2020).

Many *fangyi* have a lid. The lid often assumes a particular roof form that is called a *si'e* roof 四阿顶. Recorded in *Kaogong ji* 考工记, the people in the Shang dynasty (c. 1600–1046 BCE) built their houses with a double eave and *si'e* roof 殷人重屋 ... 四阿重屋.[9] A *si'e* roof is formed by five ridges: one lies horizontally on the top and four slope down to the four eave corners, thereby creating four sloping roof surfaces which can guide rainwater down. This type of roof was only allowed by law to apply to the royal palaces and great temples, representing the highest social status. On the roof-like lid of *fangyi*, there is always a chimney-like handle which, interestingly, also assumes a *si'e* roof form. Following the same architectural rhetoric, both the lid handle and the lid took a *si'e* form likely imitating the double-eave roof of a great hall, signifying the importance of *fangyi*. In the case of the *oufangyi*, due to the oblong shape of the lid and perhaps also the greater weight, the number of handles was doubled.

Unlike many *fangyi*, there is a unique feature on the *oufangyi*. On the two long edges of the lid, there are seven protruding parts. On the one side (likely the front side), the seven protruding parts with an appearance of small lids assume square shapes. On the other side, the seven protruding parts are of triangular shape. In line with the lid, the oblong opening of the *oufangyi* also has 14 small protruding troughs, seven on each long side. The seven troughs in the front side are squares in plan and semicircles in elevation (Figure 1.4). On the back side, the seven troughs are of triangular shape in plan (Figure 1.5). One theory from archaeology is that these troughs are designed for placing wine ladles.[10] Presumably, small wine ladles would be placed with their heads in the square troughs and their handles in the triangular troughs. Although different in size, some bronze ladles from the Shang and Zhou dynasties, with their round head and pointed end, seem to confirm this theory (see Figure 1.6).[11]

Despite its wine-related function, the relationship between the *oufangyi* and architecture is articulated in the archaeological report, as it states:

> This utensil looks grand and elegant. When the lid is put on, the upper proportion of the vessel is similar to the upper structure of a great hall. The orderly positioned seven square troughs are like the rafters of a building. Most likely this vessel was made by mimicking the great palace hall at that time.[12]

---

9 A book arguably from the pre-Qin dynasty (before 221 BCE) that was used to guide the handicraft trades, including the examination and assessment of craftsmen, see *Kaogong ji* (Shanghai, 2012), 112–116.

10 Li Qin, *Fu Hao xiaozun* (Zhengzhou, 2017), 17.

11 For the types of the bronze ladles, see Zhu Fenghan, *Gudai Zhongguo qingtong qi* (Tianjin, 1995), 251, fig. 3.63.

12 The Institute of Archaeology CASS, *Yinxu Fu Hao mu* (Beijing, 1980), 50.

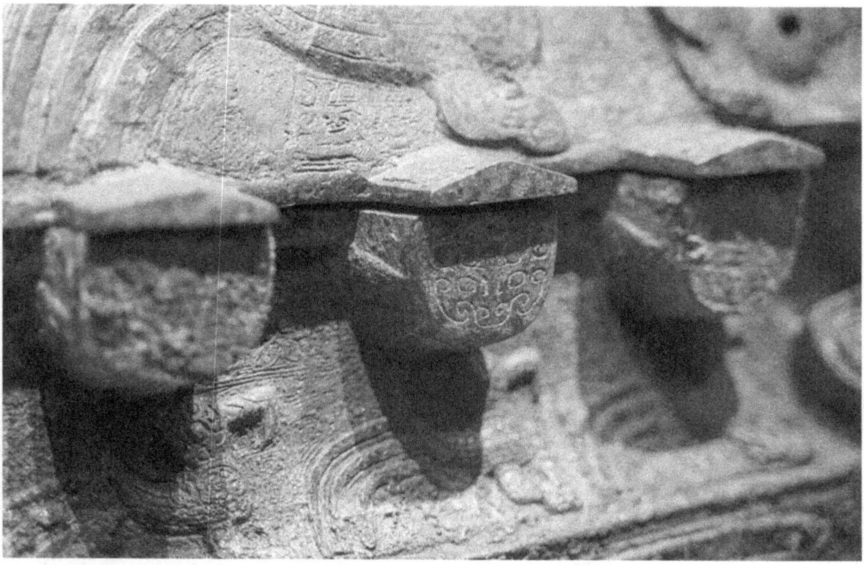

Figure 1.4 Detail of the semicircular troughs on the *oufangyi* (National Museum, photo by Fu Ruixue, 2019).

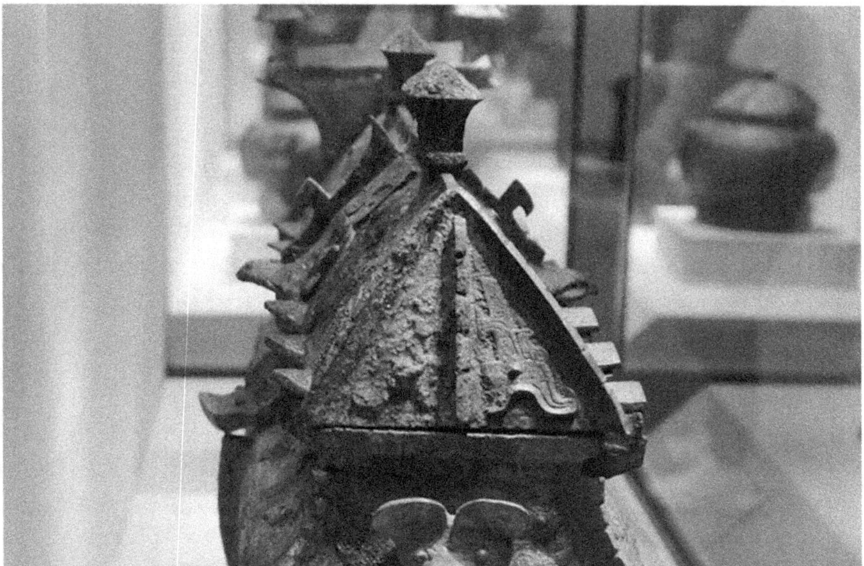

Figure 1.5 Detail of the small triangular and square lids on the two sides of the *oufangyi* (National Museum, Beijing, author's photo, 2020).

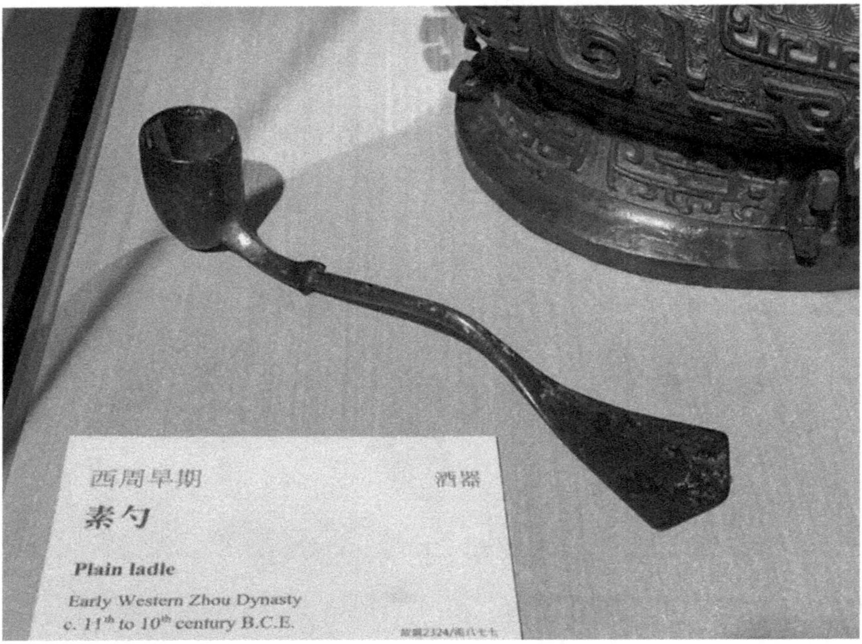

Figure 1.6 A bronze ladle with a round head and a pointed end from the eleventh to tenth centuries BCE (Taipei Palace Museum, author's photo, 2019).

The archaeological discovery of this particular vessel appears attractive to some Chinese architectural historians. Fu Xinian, for example, has carefully drawn a perspective of the *oufangyi* in an architectural fashion and studied the proportional relationship between the roof-like lid and the semicircular troughs. Fu points out that the size of the troughs is larger than that of rafters in relation to an architectural scale, and the row of the troughs is denser than that of beams, so these troughs are more likely reflecting oblique beams (*xieliang* 斜梁). To support his theory, Fu has also reviewed the different texts referring to oblique beams in the literature from the Han and Tang dynasties.[13]

Fu's assumption of likening the troughs to oblique beams under eaves seems to corroborate Yang Hongxun's theory regarding the origin of the *dougong* system. In Yang's diagram of structural transformation (see Figure 1.1), the original vertical post supporting the eave evolved into an oblique beam, denoting a significant stage that ushered in the birth of the *dougong* system.

13 Fu Xinian, *Jianzhu shi lunwen xuan* (Tianjin, 2009), 60–62.

Yet Yang's theory is questioned by Liu Tianyang who has investigated the origin of *dougong* and its early development and who believes that there is an inherent connection between *dougong* and protruding beam-heads that support an eave. To Liu, the transformation from oblique post to horizontal bracket arm, as proposed by Yang, is not structurally logical, because the supporting strength of the horizontal bracket arm is much less than that of an oblique beam. Moreover, Liu also argues that there is no evidence provided by Yang regarding the transformation stage from oblique post or curved arm (attached to the column) to horizontal bracket arm with block (*dougong* attached to the column). Liu thus claims that a protruding beam-head holding an eave is the archetype of the *dougong* system.[14] Such a viewpoint was in fact raised earlier by Liu Dunzhen in 1931, who stated that the birth of *dougong* was based on the structural development of the beam-head, appearing as a protruding part of the beam running across a column.[15] In the 1950s, Luo Zhewen also pointed out that the earliest *dougong* could be found under the corners or the edges of eaves of a building and constructed by using a natural log laying horizontally as a cantilever beam. This was the most simple and natural solution that the craftsmen would have considered in the first place.[16]

Returning to the *oufangyi*, Fu Xinian refutes the affinity between the troughs and beams (or rafters), only because the proportional relation between the troughs and the lid differs from that between the beams (or rafters) and eaves in architecture.[17] This reason seems unconvincing. The fundamental function of the *oufangyi*, as discussed earlier, was to serve as a wine container. In this case, its physical and architectural resemblance could be figurative rather than precisely mimicked. Similar to the metamorphic nature of Shang decorative art, as Wu Hung points out, there was "a painstaking effort to create metaphors for an intermediate state between the supernatural and reality—something that one could depict but not portray."[18]

Nonetheless, it is certain that the *oufangyi* captured some architectural features. Taking the square troughs, for example, their semicircular heads in elevation appeared just like logs whose upper parts have been chopped off to fit the horizontal line of an eave (see Figures 1.2 and 1.4).

---

14 Liu Tianyang, "Shilun dougong chutiao de qiyuan yu zaoqi fazhan," *Human Culture Heritage Preservation*, 2016(00):115–121.

15 The essay was originally published in *Zhongguo yingzao xueshe huikan*, 1932, 3(1), see Liu Dunzhen, *Liu Dunzhen wenji* (vol. 1) (Beijing, 1982), 36.

16 Luo Zhewen, "Dougong," *Wenwu cankao ziliao*, 1954(07):44–61.

17 Fu, *Jianzhu shi lunwen xuan*, 61.

18 Wu, *Monumentality in Early Chinese Art and Architecture*, 53.

This reflects an architectural setting in which an eave was supported by either protruding beams or rafters, and as a visible element, the beam-heads or rafter-heads would be articulated in a frontal façade of great hall.

The similarity between the *oufangyi* and architectural pattern suggests that protruding beam-heads (or rafter-heads) under an eave were the most distinctive feature of great halls in the Shang dynasty. It is also highly possible that beam-heads (or rafter-heads) were decorated with patterns similar to those on the face of the troughs (see Figure 1.4). Following Luo and Liu's theories, the detailed portrait of the square troughs in the *oufangyi* logically indicates the origin of the *dougong* system (i.e., beam-head or rafter-head) in terms of its structural function. The decorative nature of the troughs, and of beam-heads/rafter-heads in architecture, also anticipated a period when the rich forms and ornaments of the *dougong* system were developed.

The Bronze Vessel with Columns and Blocks

If the representation of the *dougong* system in the *oufangyi* seems tentative, then that in the following case is significantly more definite. In a bronze vessel from the Western Zhou period (c. 1045–771 BCE) unearthed from Luoyang in 1929, the forms of *dou* (block) and column are clearly incorporated into its four legs (Figure 1.7). It is one of a pair of two identical bronze vessels. They are called *celing gui* 夨令簋, also a type of wine container but without a lid. Archeologists interpreted the 110 characters inscribed in the interior of the vessel on its base, as revealing the events of war, ritual ceremony, awards

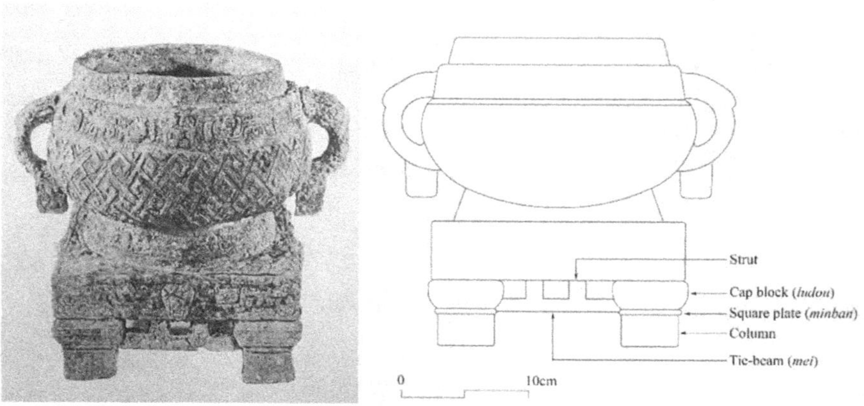

Figure 1.7 The *celing gui* and its elevation (from Rong Geng and Zhang Weichi, *Yin Zhou qingtong qi tonglun*, fig. 27, plate 52; author's drawing on the right).

and banquets that related to the making of this vessel.[19] Some scholars assert that the vessel was made during the reign of the Zhou king Chengwang 周成王 (1042–1021 BCE), while others believe it was made during Zhaowang's reign 周昭王 (?–977 BCE).[20] According to Yi Hongbing, the Zhou king Zhaowang launched a series of wars against the southern region, their main purpose being to pillage copper resources. As recorded in the bronze inscription, in Zhaowang's fist conquest, a large amount of copper was plundered, which was then appropriated by many aristocrats to make bronze vessels cerebrating the victory.[21] Indeed, copper was a critical strategic resource in the Chinese Bronze Age as K. C. Chang points out, and he adds that bronze vessels played a central role in political campaigns during that time.[22]

Other than its political and ritual importance, the *celing gui* has an extra pedestal that is exceptionally architectural compared to other *gui* so far unearthed. This has also drawn architectural historians' attention. As a chief editor, Liu Dunzhen provided a line drawing of the *celing gui* in the *History of Ancient Chinese Architecture* 中国古代建筑史, the architectural textbook for higher education in China. The related text explains that bronze vessels from the Western Zhou period often reflect some architectural details. The four legs of the *celing gui*, for example, were made into the form of a square column. There are four cap blocks (*ludong* 栌斗) on the top of each column connected by four tie beams, and two struts on each tie beam. Resembling an architectural structure, this pedestal supports the square base of the *celing gui*. Considering the time of its making as indicated by archaeologists, the architectural editorial team conjectures that the *ludong* (cap block) emerged in the late Shang dynasty, while the *gong* (bracket arm) appeared thereafter.[23]

Working as an assistant to Liu Dunzhen, Fu Xinian had also been involved in the editorial work of the *History of Ancient Chinese Architecture* from 1963 to 1965. Later on, in his own research on the architecture of the Western Zhou period, Fu provided more details of his analysis of the *celing gui*. In particular, Fu observes that there is a ridge in between the column and cap block indicated by the bronze form. This resembles a square plate (*minban* 皿板) often placed at the bottom of a block (*dou*). This detail is evident in the architecture of the Han dynasty and thereafter.[24] In traditional Chinese wooden architecture,

19 Chen Mengjia, *Xi Zhou tongqi duandai* (Beijing, 2004), 29–31.
20 Fu, *Jianzhu shi lunwen xuan*, 54.
21 Yi Hongbing, "Zhou Zhaowang nanzheng duixiang kao," *Renwen zazhi*, 2008(02): 159–163.
22 K. C. Chang, *Zhongguo qingtong shidai* (Beijing, 1999), 36.
23 Liu Dunzhen, *Zhongguo gudai jianzhu shi* (Beijing, 1984), 39.
24 Fu, *Jianzhu shi lunwen xuan*, 54.

such a plate or *minban* was used to increase the surface connection between a cap block and column, thereby enhancing the stability of the structure. It also prevents the moisture traveling upward, providing a means of damp proofing. Researchers further point out that a *minban* plate could also help to adjust the height difference among the columns and ensure that beams were level.[25] This subtle nuanced feature *minban* in the bronze vessel reinforces that the pedestal of the *celing gui* has truthfully reflected *dougong* system in architecture. Judging from the architectural details on the pedestal of the *celing gui*, it seems to be quite valid for Fu to claim that the major buildings in the Western Zhou period employed *dou* (block) on their columns and the columns, tie beams, and struts would be processed into rectilinear forms.[26]

The Bronze Table and Corner Bracket Set

In the research on early forms of *dougong*, a bronze table unearthed from the royal tomb of Zhongshan state (414–296 BCE) during the Warring States period (481/403–221 BCE) provides a classical example (Figure 1.8). Some

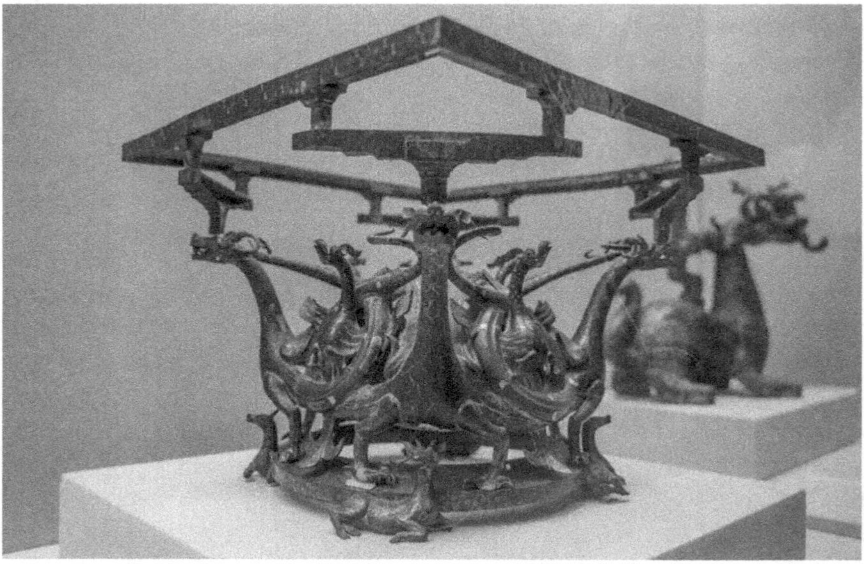

Figure 1.8 The bronze table stand, unearthed from the royal tomb of Zhongshan state (414–296 BCE) (exhibited in the National Museum, Beijing, photo by Fu Ruixue, 2019).

25 Zhang Yijie, Li Yin, and Han Xiao, "The Origin of the Pu-Pai-Fang (Plate)," *Huazhong Architecture*, 2018(5):118–120.

26 Fu, *Jianzhu shi lunwen xuan*, 55.

47.5 cm in length, 47 cm in width, and 36.2 cm in height, this bronze table has wavy patterns of gold and silver inlay, and consists of four dragons, four phoenixes, and four deer.[27] Presumably made with timber originally, the tabletop had decayed and only the bronze stand survived, with a circular bottom and a square top. The transformation from the bottom circle to the top square was elaborately achieved through introducing animal motifs. There are four sika deer reclining on the bottom ring. Four dragons, each with two legs, stand on the ring, with their tails curving up connecting their horns. The two wings of each dragon lean inward and upward, with the eight forming a small circular space in the center. In the intervening spaces between two dragons, there are four flying phoenixes. Each dragon head supports the square top through a unique bracket set, that is, a post with cap block braces a horizontal arm, on which stood two struts with cap blocks bracketing the square frame (Figure 1.9).

For a piece of furniture, the bracket sets on the four corners seem to be redundant. Logically, each dragon body could be further stretched and its head directly connected to each corner of the square frame. In addition, as a rigid structural part, the corner bracket sets seem not to match the organic faunal forms beneath. To employ the architectural vocabulary to the furniture, it perhaps fulfilled a metaphor, that is, the bronze table was a miniature of great hall. Through emphasizing the cantilevered corner, it is likened to the square top of the four eaves of a roof, that is, the most prestigious roof

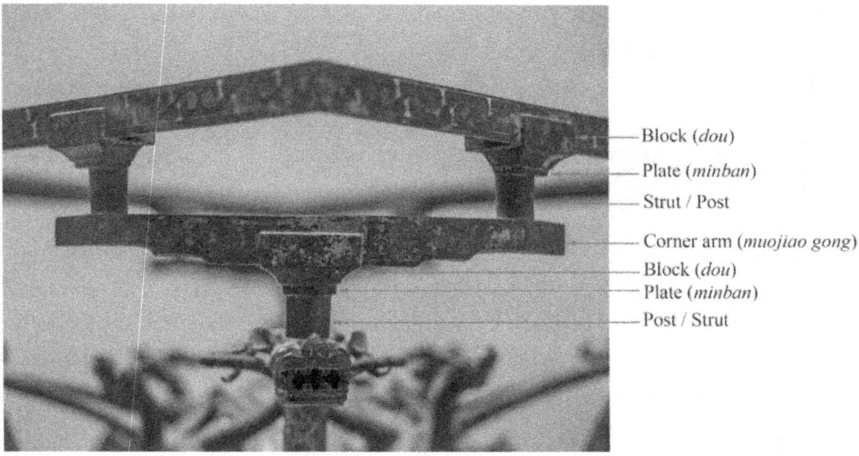

Figure 1.9 The corner bracket set on the bronze table stand (photo by Fu Ruixue, 2019, author's annotation).

27 Yang Jie, "Cuo jinyin silong sifeng tongfangan jianshang," *World of Antiquity*, 2014(6):72–74.

form *si'e*, aforementioned. It is unclear whether the invention of the corner bracket set was driven by esthetic reasons to articulate overhanging eaves as a structural innovation, or whether it was to showcase the unification of curved organic form and squared mechanical form. Perhaps there was even an economic consideration in removing corner columns supporting eaves. The cantilevered eaves at the four corners would enable people to perambulate around the building under their cover more readily, without the obstacle of corner columns. Moreover, by replacing corner columns with bracket sets, there was no chance for rain to splash the wooden corner columns.

These exquisite details of the bracket set—the *dougong* system—suggest that the craftsmanship involved in making such a *dougong* system was quite mature and elegant at that time. This led Fu Xinian to claim that the *dougong* system in wooden architecture appeared much earlier than the time when this bronze table was made.[28] To Fu, the square frame at the top of the stand resembles a square roof; the dragon head and body are like a bracket arm protruding from a corner column.[29] In between, there are layers of elements comprising a corner *dougong* system, including a post with cap block, a corner bracket arm, two struts with blocks, and an eave corner, in an upward sequence (Figure 1.9).

Similarly, Yang Hongxun believes that the upper corner of the bronze stand mirrors architectural craftsmanship. The dragon head and body can be seen as a curved bracket arm, protruding as if from a vertical column at 45 degrees. Yang uses a particular term *luan* 栾 (curved bracket arm) from the Han literature to describe this curved bracket arm. To Yang, the wooden structural parts, such as columns, beams, and bracket arms, in the Pre-Qin period (before 221 BCE) were often excessively decorated and bronze ornamentation was widely applied. Particularly, *luan* was often decorated with a dragon pattern and most likely *luan* itself could be made into a bronze dragon.[30]

There are abundant physical remains from the Han dynasty, such as stone architecture, reliefs, and pottery models, all of which indicate the widespread use of curved bracket arms. Some bracket arms were carved as dragons. These findings perhaps provide a firm ground for Yang's theoretical assertion above. Yet there is also solid evidence suggesting that curved bracket arms on columns appeared earlier at a similar time to that of the bronze table. For example, lacquerware unearthed from Linzi (Shandong Province), produced in between the late Spring and Autumn period (c. 771–476 BCE)

---

28 Fu, *Jianzhu shi lunwen xuan*, 79.

29 Ibid.

30 Yang, "Dougong qiyuan kaocha," in: *Jianzhu kaoguxue lunwenji*, 260–261.

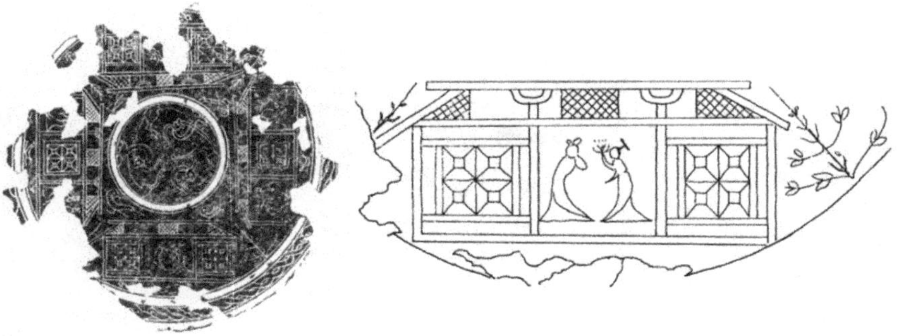

Figure 1.10 Housing motif on lacquerware unearthed from Linzi, Shandong Province (after *Kaogu xuebao*, 1(1977):73–104, fig. 14; author's drawing enlarged on the right).

and the early Warring States period, shows four similar houses arranged at the four cardinal points within a circle. In each house, illustrated by the elevation diagram, there are two columns with a curved bracket arm above, holding the ridgepole (Figure 1.10).

Uniting the curved organic animal forms and rectilinear tabletop in the bronze table, and connecting the curved bracket arm to a linear ridgepole in the lacquerware illustration, both cases indicate similar concepts and attempt to reconcile an esthetic struggle between a rectilinear form and a curvilinear one. The struggle seems to have achieved a satisfactory outcome in that a mature form of *dougong* appeared in the later dynasties, which offers a perfect solution to unify linear and curved forms: a square block supported by a curved arm.

Bronzes and Religious Buildings

Considering most bronze utensils were confined to early great halls, the linkage between bronze utensils and architecture seems to be inherent to a certain degree. A dialectic relationship existed between bronze utensils and their architectural context that has been articulated by Wu Hung, as he states: "sacred bronzes gave meaning and authority to temple, but these bronzes became functional and meaningful only during temple rituals."[31] In a number of bronze utensils unearthed from the Western Zhou period, scenes of ritual ceremony are evident (Figures 1.11–1.13).

31 Wu, *Monumentality in Early Chinese Art and Architecture*, 78.

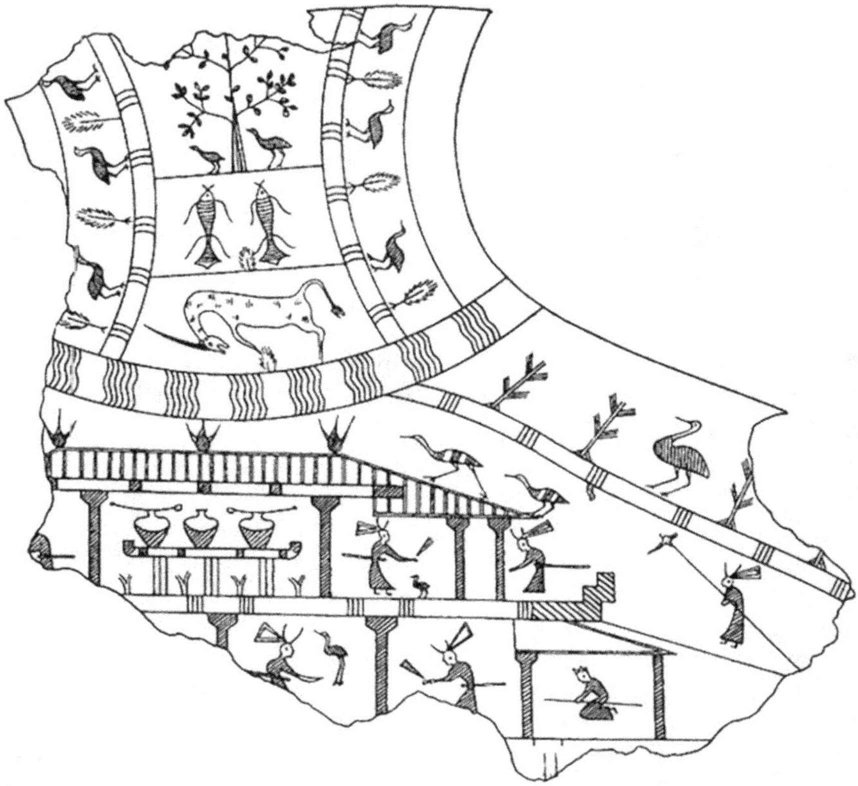

Figure 1.11 Redrawing of the decoration on a bronze vase from the Warring States period, unearthed from Changye, Shanxi Province (source: *Kaogu*, 1(1957), 109, fig. 2).

Charles D. Weber has discussed these pictorial bronzes in great detail and he also confirms that the dates of their production range from the sixth to fifth centuries BCE.[32] These scenes often consist of a religious building presented in elevation or section with a symmetrical layout, two or three large wine vessels placed in a central position either on a table or on the floor, sometimes with ladles, and shamans performing their rites with different postures.

It seems that the three bronzes discussed earlier, that is, the building-like *oufangyi*, the *celing gui* with four legs resembling columns and blocks, and the bronze table with corner bracket sets, would be naturally associated with a building for ritual ceremony in their respective historic period. In line with the buildings that enshrined them, these bronzes might have served similar

32 Weber, "Chinese Pictorial Bronze Vessels of the Late Chou Period, Part II," *Artibus Asiae*, 1966, vol. 28(4), 271–311.

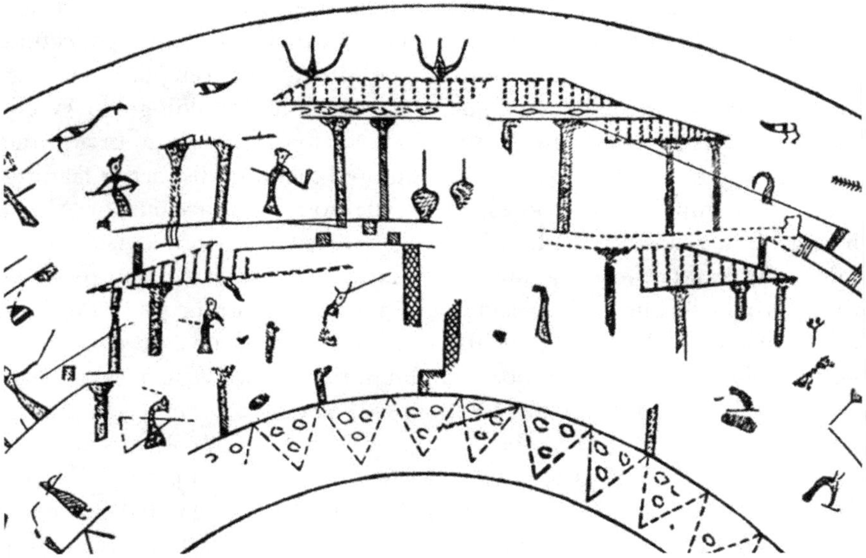

Figure 1.12 Redrawing of the decoration on a bronze basin from the Warring States period, unearthed from Hui County, Henan Province (source: The Institute of Archaeology CASS, *Huixian fajue baogao* (Beijing, 1956), 116, fig. 138).

c

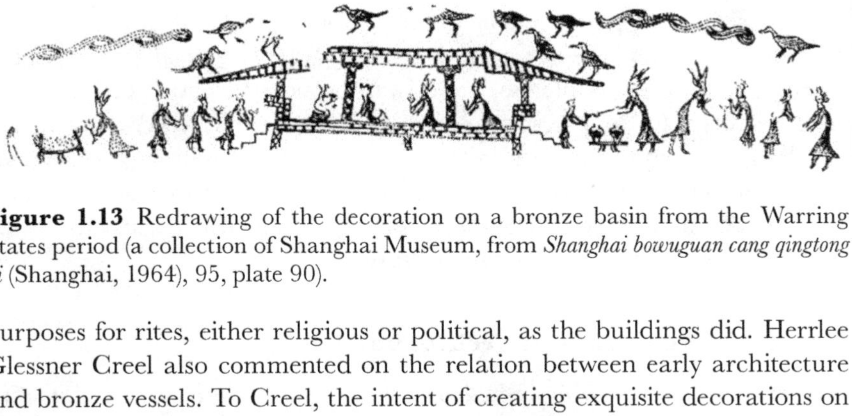

Figure 1.13 Redrawing of the decoration on a bronze basin from the Warring States period (a collection of Shanghai Museum, from *Shanghai bowuguan cang qingtong qi* (Shanghai, 1964), 95, plate 90).

purposes for rites, either religious or political, as the buildings did. Herrlee Glessner Creel also commented on the relation between early architecture and bronze vessels. To Creel, the intent of creating exquisite decorations on bronzes could possibly be applied to the architecture too, as he states that:

> Concerning the interior decoration of these buildings we have little direct evidence. But even if we had none it would be safe to infer that the creators of the Shang bronzes and sculptures did not leave their halls of state and temples without suitable adornment.[33]

33 Creel, *The Birth of China*, 66.

More tangible is the link between the three bronzes and the illustrated religious buildings described above in terms of their reflected architectural forms. In the engraved scenes depicting rituals, the religious buildings are the focal point of the ceremony. The illustrated buildings, to Weber, "must be considered an attempted reconstruction rather than an accurate presentation."[34] Yet they have vividly captured the most distinctive features, such as columns, beams, floors, and roof, from early architecture. First, in the building shown in Figure 1.11, as Weber points out, "the hatched squares under the roof between the major columns of the top floor may represent the ends of tie beams."[35] This detail highlights the importance of beam-heads in the facade of a building, articulated much earlier in the *oufangyi*. Second, all the columns in those religious buildings, to borrow Weber's words, "are topped with expanded capitals, but there are no brackets."[36] It is clear in these illustrated buildings that cap blocks appear on the top of columns and they assume either rectangular or wedge shapes in elevation (see Figures 1.11–1.13). Similar architectural features of column and cap block were well documented in the *celing gui*. Third, all the illustrated buildings have overhanging eaves, which are supported either by two small columns (Figures 1.11 and 1.12) or by a post standing on the top of a parapet (Figure 1.13). These truly reflect the architectural solutions for the four corners of eaves during the fifth and sixth centuries BCE, prior to the invention of the corner bracket set as suggested by the bronze table (414–296 BCE). The three bronzes, as examples *par excellence*, also illustrate a logical evolvement of the *dougong* form in architecture, that is, from the articulation of beam-head in the *oufangyi* to the emergence of the square block in the *celing gui*, then reaching the mature expression of a corner bracket set as in the bronze table. If the connection between the bronze pieces and architecture discussed above is seen only as indirect, then the following section will discuss the direct application of bronze items in architecture.

Bronze Components in Architecture

The practice of employing bronze as a structural component in architecture is also noticeable in early China. As with the cases discussed above, the bronze components will also be presented in chronological order of the time they were produced, rather than their discovery dates and associated literature publication dates in modern times.

---

34 Weber, "Chinese Pictorial Bronze Vessels of the Late Chou Period, Part II," 275.

35 Ibid., 278.

36 Ibid.

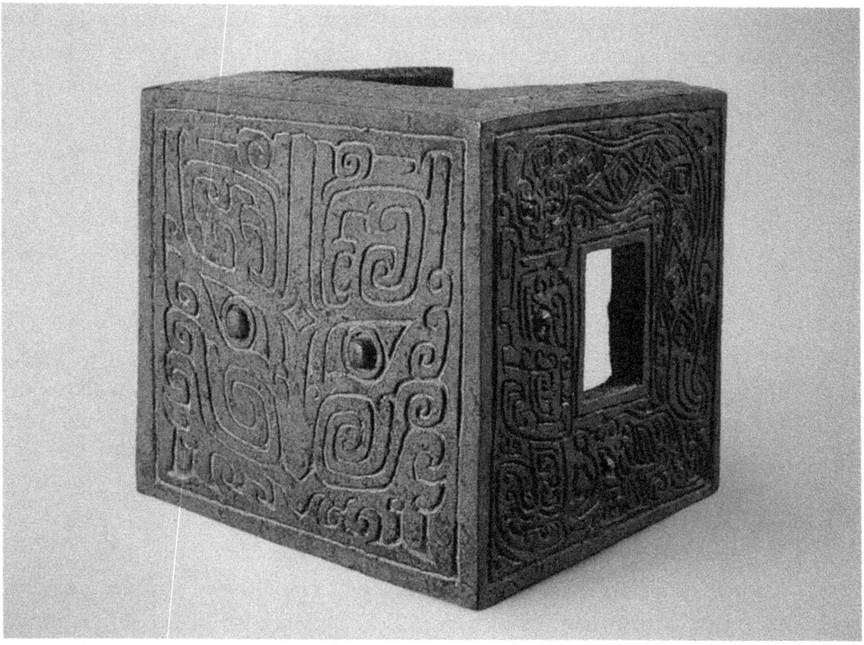

Figure 1.14 The bronze box fitting from the Shang dynasty discovered in the Xiaoshuangqiao site, Henan Province (Henan Museum, Zhengzhou, author's photo, 2021).

Two similar bronze ornaments were discovered in 1985 and 1989, respectively, in the Xiaoshuangqiao archaeological site, Henan Province. Each one has a box form, with walls on the front and two sides. There is a rectangular hole on each side wall, allowing a wooden or metal pin to be inserted as a fastener. One of the bronze ornaments remains in very good condition (Figure 1.14). With a weight of 6 kg, the size of this bronze ornament is 18.5 cm in height, with a width of 18.8 cm for its front wall and 16.5 cm for its side walls. The size of the two rectangular holes is 6 cm × 4.2 cm.[37]

In the Xiaoshuangqiao site, there are many relics of palace buildings from the Middle Shang period (c. 1400–1350 BCE). Associated with those building relics, the two bronze ornaments are the earliest architectural fittings discovered so far. Judging by their physical setting, these bronze ornaments are assumed to be a sheath for a beam-head, cast with the purpose of

37 For more details, see Henan Provincial Antiquities Institute, ed., *Zhengzhou Shang cheng kaogu xin faxian yu yanjiu* (Zhengzhou, 1993), 242–271.

protection and decoration.[38] In reviewing the possible ways of its installation, Yang Hongxun opposes the above theory that links the bronze fitting to a beam-head, mainly because the position of beam-head, far above eye level, prevents its three-side decoration from being revealed.[39] The uncertainty of the location and function of the bronze fitting in architecture has led to a heated debate among archaeologists. Indeed, if it was not at the beam-head, then where would the bronze ornament precisely fit? Following Yang's theory, Song Guoding thus proposes that the bronze fitting would be fixed in the front of a door bearing, possibly as a part of door socket, on the two sides of a doorway. In such a position, the three-sided decoration plus the comparatively refined top edge would be properly visible to human eyes. In addition, the two side walls of the fitting show a skewed shape in elevation. This, to Song, suggests that the bottom part would fit on a slightly slopping ground next to a doorsill which was designed for drainage purposes.[40]

Song's theory is, however, challenged by Zheng Jiexiang. Through surveying the relevant literature from early China, Zheng claims that there was a common practice among the wealthier households to have a post in the middle of a doorway, such post being called *menjue* 门橛. In a central position, the bronze fitting would be placed on the ground to act as a base for the centralized post.[41] Elizabeth Childs-Johnson has also studied the bronze ornament and mentioned that a third one was found in 1992 that has disappeared. To Childs-Johnson, the bronze ornaments were unlikely to be used as door sockets which were created out of stone and were circular. Considering their size and shape, Childs-Johnson believes that "these three bronze fittings, with hard-edged U-shapes on the interior probably held either two upright rectangular posts of a door or something similar in size."[42]

Most likely due to the unpolished bottom of the bronze fitting, both Song and Zheng's assumptions are based on the solution of concealing the base by connecting it to the ground. However, quiet recently, Zhang Junru has questioned these theories from Chinese scholars. Considering the hollowing space of the bronze fitting (about 18.5 cm × 12 cm) that is only suitable for a rectangular piece of wood, this, to Zhang, is unfit for a major beam-head. Placing the bronze fitting on the ground, either on two sides or in the middle of

38 Song Guoding, "Bronze Ornaments for Buildings in the Earlier Shang Period and Related Problems," in: *Zhengzhou Shang cheng kaogu xin faxian yu yanjiu*, 74.

39 Ibid.

40 Ibid., 75.

41 Zheng Jiexiang, "The discussion of the function of the bronze architectural fitting from the Xiaoshuangqiao site," *Gudai wenming yanjiu tongxun*, 2008(38):28–31.

42 Elizabeth Childs-Johnson, "Urban daemons of early Shang: Urbanism in ancient China," *Archaeological Research in Asia*, June 2018(14):137.

a doorway, is also unreasonable, because either would impair the visibility of its three-sided decoration. Zhang believes that the protruding square head of a tie beam crossing through a column would be an ideal spot for this bronze fitting.[43]

Robert L. Thorp has also commented on the bronze fitting though he may have been unfamiliar with the debate regarding the possible location of the fitting. Thorp's comments are rather general, stating that:

> These fittings were probably applied over the exposed end of a square wooden beam [...]. Very little hardware like this has been associated with Shang buildings, although Zhou-period examples are known and the practice continued into later times.[44]

The exact position of this bronze fitting in architecture remains inconclusive. Yet it seems to be certain that this bronze fitting would be a head piece for any rectangular wooden structural element with a connected space approximately 18.5 cm × 15 cm × 12 cm. It would be placed in a suitable position to reveal its three-side decoration (Figure 1.15).

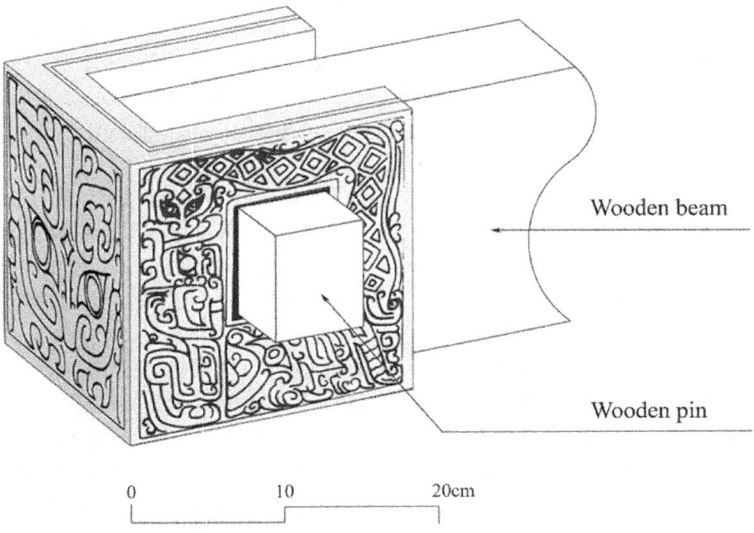

Figure 1.15 The possible installation of the bronze box fitting over the wooden structures (author's drawings, 2020).

43 Zhang Junru, "Shoumianwen qingtong jianzhu goujian," online.

44 Robert Thorp, *China in the Early Bronze Age: Shang Civilization* (Philadelphia, 2006), 83.

One later historic account probably provides a clue to the location of the bronze fitting. *Guliang zhuan* 穀梁传 (a commentary on the Confucian Classic *Chunqiu*), records that in 670 BCE, square rafters termed as *jue* 桷 were commonly produced for buildings of the upper classes. For royal palace buildings, the rafters would be cut into a square form and polished by fine grindstone. For the buildings of dukes and princes, the rafters would be similarly processed into a square form but roughly polished. The rafters for officials' buildings were cut into a square form without any polish. Scholars' buildings could only have the rafter heads chopped so that they would be aligned.[45] This clearly suggests that the rafters were a visible and preeminent element of a building symbolizing social hierarchy. The penchant for processing natural round rafters into square ones was codified by law, and the most prestigious form was the highly refined square rafter. In this regard, would the square bronzing fitting be a head piece for a rafter? Although the two cases are about 700 years apart, the late practice of squaring round rafters could possibly have originated from the early treatment of rafter head, by cutting it into a square form covered with a bronze ornament. This theory can be partially verified through comparing the square bronzing fitting with the *oufangyi*. As discussed earlier, the troughs on the *oufangyi* reflect either protruding beam-heads or rafter-heads under an eave, revealing a distinctive feature of Shang great halls. Not only are the two bronze pieces from the same dynasty, but the decoration pattern (i.e., *taotie*, monster mask) on the front of the trough is similar to that on the front wall of this bronze fitting (see Figures 1.4 and 1.14).

In Yinxu where the relics of the Late Shang (c. 1350–1046 BCE) buildings were concentrated, archaeologists have also discovered 11 bronze column plinths consisting of two major types at a building foundation: one is a circular plinth with a diameter of 10–15 cm (Figure 1.16) while the other consists of bronze plates of different shapes, being placed on the top of stone bases. With a curved and elegant profile, the former also plays an ornamental role, on top of which a column of 10–15 cm diameter can be assumed.[46] Considering the size of these columns, they were most likely employed as posts supporting eaves. Such size also indicates that columns and beams supporting the lower (or secondary) eave of a great hall were comparatively small. In this regard, the bronze fitting aforementioned seems to fit well on a beam-head or column cap.

45 Guliang Chi, *Chunqiu Guliang zhuan zhushu*, ch. 6, 68–69.

46 Shang-Zhou archaeology team of the Department of History, Peking University, ed., *Shang Zhou kaogu* (Beijing, 1979), 69.

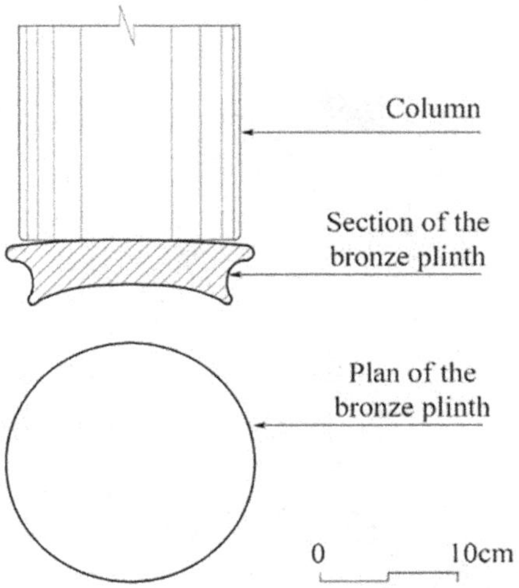

Figure 1.16 The drawing of the bronze column plinth unearthed in the palace relics of Yinxu, Anyang, Henan Province (author's drawing, 2020, based on *Shang Zhou kaogu* (Beijing, 1979), 69, fig. 46).

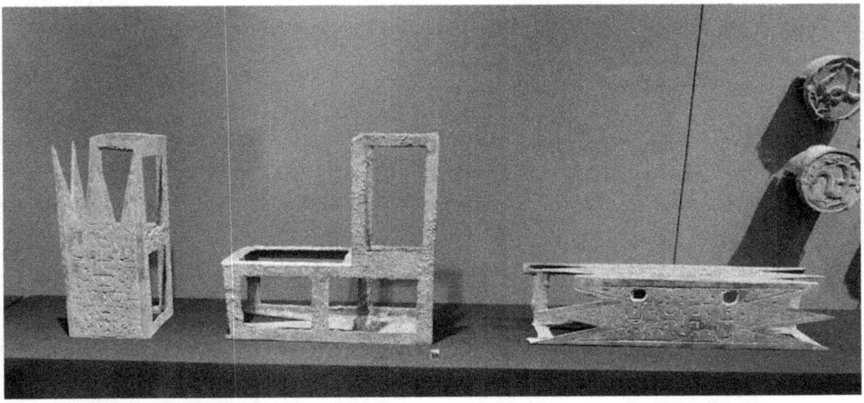

Figure 1.17 Three of the 64 bronze structural members unearthed in the Fengxiang site, Shaanxi Province (Shaanxi History Museum, Xi'an, author's photo, 2021).

Since 1973, 64 pieces of bronze items have been excavated from the relic of Yongcheng, a capital city of the Qin state (677–383/374 BCE) during the Spring and Autumn period (Figure 1.17).[47] Yang Hongxun believes these

47 Fengxiang County Cultural Centre and Shaanxi Provincial Committee for Management of Cultural and Historical Relics, "Fengxiang xian Qin gongdian shijue ji tongzhi jianzhu goujian," *Kaogu*, 1976(2):121–132.

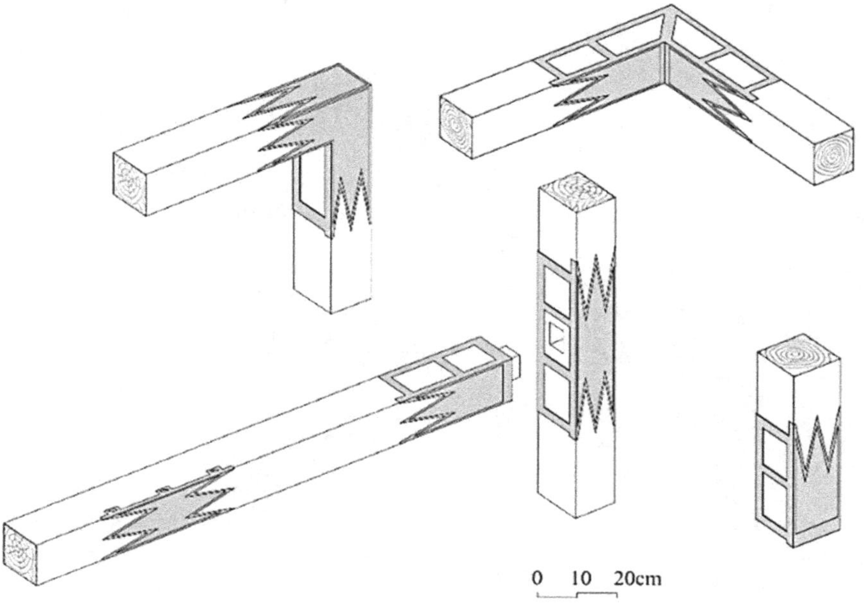

Figure 1.18 The possible installations for the bronze structural members on wooden structures (author's drawing, 2020).

bronze items were structural components in early architecture, and he uses a particular term *gang* 釭 from the early literature to define them (Figure 1.18). There is concrete evidence from the archaeological finding that supports Yang's conclusion: (1) the large bronze items were fittings for wooden structures, because they contained rotten wood when excavated; (2) The hollow spaces within the large items are mostly square, measuring 16 cm × 16 cm. This size of wood is much larger than that used for carriages and furniture and must be architectural components; (3) The sizes of the wooden structures suggested by the large bronze items are smaller than those used for major structural work in buildings (e.g., columns and beams), so these bronze items were most likely used for pilasters and tie beams on the wall; and (4) Judging from the size and type of these bronze items, they perfectly match the size of wooden components on pilasters and tie beams, and they also suggest a possible (or logical) way of installation.[48] To further validate his claims, Yang has also examined the meanings of *gang* in some of the Han literature describing architecture, and his findings confirm that *gang*, as a metal fitting

48 Yang Hongxun, "Fengxiang chutu Chunqiu Qin gong tonggou-jingang," *Kaogu*, 1976(02):103–108.

for reinforcement and decoration, was widely applied to the wooden structure of the Han palace buildings.[49]

A piece of bronze ornament was unearthed in Luyuan, Jiangsu Province, in 1972 (Figure 1.19). It is in a complete form of a *dougong*, with an overall length of 62 cm and height of 38 cm. On the top, there is a square block

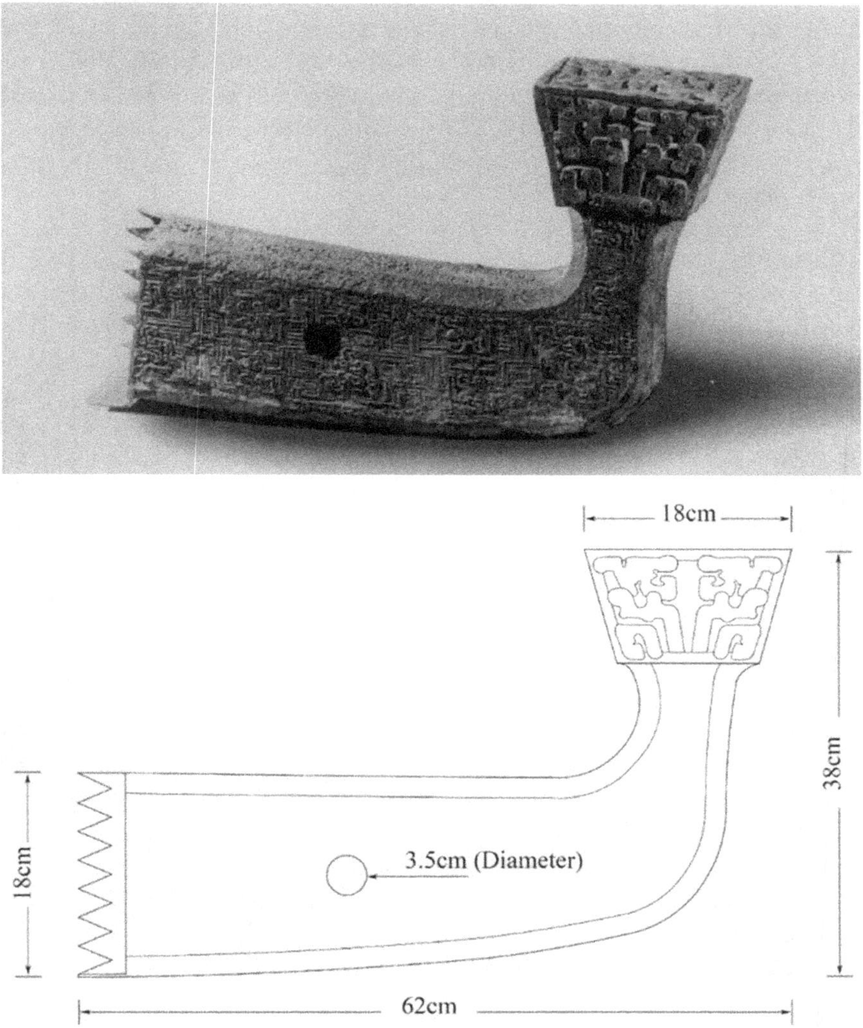

Figure 1.19 The bronze *dougong* from the eighth to thirteenth centuries BCE unearthed from Luyuan, Jiangsu Province (photo courtesy of Nanjing Museum; author's drawing, 2020).

49 Ibid.

which is supported by a curved arm. The square block is hollowed out with the pattern of a curled serpent and auspicious clouds. A similar decorative pattern is also applied to the curved arm which is hollow inside too. At the end of the curved arm, there are seven sawtooth serving to grip a structural piece that could be inserted into the arm. There is a hole with a diameter of 3.5 cm located in the middle of the curved arm, though only on one side. This is for a pin to fasten the inserted item. According to the archaeologist Zou Houben, after scrutinizing the excavation site of this bronze ornament, not much evidence for other relevant cultural relics could be found. Judging from the patterns on pieces of pottery from the same period, this bronze ornament was probably made between the Spring and Autumn period and the Warring States period.[50]

As a particular fitting, such hollowed bronze ornament is called *gang* 釭. The term *gang* appeared widely in the literature from the Han dynasty. In *Shuowen jiezi* 说文解字, an early second-century Chinese dictionary, *gang* is a metal hub, the central part of a wheel for a carriage.[51] In the Han lexicon, *Shiming* 释名, the term *gang* appears particularly as a component of a carriage as it states: "*gang* means hollow, it is hollow inside."[52] Following these explanations, the bronze *dougong* is thus regarded as a particular part of a carriage. It would be a metal ornament for a hub, or most likely an axle end. Equipped with a metal hub, the wooden parts of a wheel would be more resistant to deformation, cracking, and being warped. Other than the functional benefit, the metal ornament would also embellish the carriage, thereby revealing the noble status of its passengers. Yet for this particular bronze *dougong*, Zou Houben proposes another theory. He believes that this bronze *dougong* was a structural member used in architecture at the time, for example, as a connection to pilasters and tie beams on walls.[53] Indeed, according to Yang Hongxun's research on the bronze structural members unearthed from Fengxiang County (Shaanxi Province), *gang* also refers to metal ornaments or fittings that were widely used in early palace buildings.

The opening in this bronze *dougong* with one side containing seven sawteeth is about 18 cm × 8 cm. These dimensions would fit neither any parts of a carriage nor any types of domestic furniture. Considering the archaeological findings, so far, there are no metal parts from early carriages that match the bronze *dougong* in size or shape. The term *gang*, referring to the metal

50 Zou Houben, "Chunqiu shengyu zhuangshi goujian," in: *The Collection Category of Nanjing Museum* (Shanghai, 1992), 162.

51 Xu Shen, *Shuowen jiezi zhu* (Shanghai, 2019), 711.

52 Liu Xi, *Shiming* (Beijing, 2016), 109.

53 Zou, "Chunqiu shengyu zhuangshi goujian," 163.

fitting for carriage wheels is in fact a cylinder piece for either hub or ornament at the both ends of an axle.[54] Therefore, the bronze *dougong* is most likely an early architectural component. Its opening size is similar to that of the box bronze fitting from the Middle Shang discussed earlier. Most likely this bronze *dougong* was installed on a column or a beam which would fundamentally resolve the structural fragility brought about by using a wooden bracket set.

The discovery of these bronze components has significantly extended our knowledge of architecture in early China. The material importance of bronze, the structural durability of metal, and the virtuosity of bronze casting craftsmanship, all would inevitably contribute to the development of wooden architecture.

Bronze Columns and Architecture

In tune with the development of bronze architectural components, bronze columns were also widely employed in religious narratives, arts, and architecture, though the relevant evidence currently remains in the literature alone. The practice of using bronze columns in palace buildings could be traced back to the Shang dynasty. According to *Shiji* 史记 (*The Grand Scribe's Records*, completed around 94 BCE), the last Shang king Zhou 纣王 (c. 1105–1045 BCE) invented a punishment called *paoluo* 炮烙, a particularly cruel way of torture.[55] The Western Han scholar Liu Xiang 刘向 (77–6 BCE) explained this punishment in his book *Lienü zhuan* 列女传, stating that the *paoluo* punishment was created by Zhou. Lying horizontally as a beam, a bronze column would be greased and heated by burning charcoals. The criminals would be forced to walk on the heated bronze column, and they would quickly fall into the burning charcoals and be seared to death.[56] Despite the primitiveness of the punishment, its invention was inevitably associated with the available material on hand, that is, bronze columns. It is safe to assume that bronze columns were precast and often used in the Shang palace halls. Although exclusive to royal palaces and great temples, this architectural tradition, as indicated by the literature above, continued well into the Han dynasty. The bronze columns appeared in the Han literature are discussed in the section 'The Earth and the Heavens' in Chapter 2.

54 Zhang Changshou, *Shang Zhou kaogu lunji* (Beijing, 2007), 231–272. For the various types of bronze fittings, particularly cylindrical *gang*, in early carriages, see Zhu, *Gudai Zhongguo qingtong qi*, 351–359, figs. 4.28–4.37.

55 Sima Qian, *Shiji* (Wuhan, 2017), 44.

56 Liu Xiang, *Lienü zhuan* (Shenyang, 1998), 73.

The bronze columns and structural components seem to have once prevailed in the great halls of early China. If the main theme of traditional Chinese architecture is dominated by wooden architecture and remains unchallengeable, then at least the use of bronze elements contributed significantly to improving the function and appearance of wooden architecture. In particular, the development of the bronze components seem to have filled a gap between the early rudimentary use of wooden joints and the later prevalence of the sophisticated *dougong* system and tenon-and-mortise work in architecture. Indeed, the discovery of the 64 pieces of bronze structural members from the Spring and Autumn period leads Yang Hongxun to claim that these bronze components not only broadened our understanding of the metal *gang* in early architecture but also have shaped the development of wooden structural joints thereafter.[57] Hou Fei further underlines that there are ten typological categories among these 64 bronze components, which, in their elaborate forms, manifest the effort and practice of standardization of technology in both architecture and bronze casting. This is a remarkable achievement in early China.[58]

Considering the bronze columns in the temple and palace halls as indicated by the literature, and their possible engagement with bronze components (e.g., the bronze *dougong*), one perhaps cannot help wondering if bronze *dougong* predated wooden *dougong* in architecture. To conventional thinking, wood as a building material is more primitive than bronze. Based on the *dougong* forms from the bronze vessels, furniture, and components, most scholars have suggested that similar forms in wooden architecture would have taken place much earlier. Yet the possibility does exist that the wide use of bronze components pre-dated the period when wooden bracket sets flourished. One particular perspective is, for example, that the curvilinear forms with exquisite decorative patterns prevailed in early bronze utensils. There were also the attempts to reconcile curvilinear forms with rectilinear ones, evident in the bronze table and in the architecture illustrated in the lacquerware, as discussed earlier. It is hard to dismiss their influence on the later development of curved bracket arms in architecture. Another perspective concerns the decoration motifs, such as masks or faces of daemons, dragons and serpents, phoenixes and birds, tigers and beasts, and auspicious clouds, all of which are widely evident on the bronze vessels and structural members from

57 Yang, "Fengxiang chutu Chunqiu Qin gong tonggou," 106.

58 Hou Fei, "The development of technological standardization in early China: The case study of the bronze fittings from the Spring and Autumn Period," *Popular Standardization*, 2014(11):52–56.

early China. Their continuity in traditional architecture is also remarkable. Yet, amazingly, the complexity and sophistication of the decorative patterns in early bronzes were never surpassed by those in wooden/stone architecture from the succeeding dynasties.

The excessive use of animal and natural/supernatural elements in early bronzes also served one fundamental purpose, that is, to establish a communication between heaven and earth. In his research on the animal motif of bronze vessels, K. C. Chang states that: “If the bronze ritual vessels were a part of the shamanistic paraphernalia in the heaven-earth crossing, it should come as no surprise that images of animals who were helpers in this task were cast on the vessels.”[59] Yet the access to heaven–earth communication was a prerequisite for political authority, as Chang points out. Indeed, as confirmed by the oracle bone inscriptions, the Shang king was the head shaman, assisted by many religious figures.[60] In this regard, the bronze pieces, the great halls of royal palaces, and religious temples would share even more essential qualities, such as having one common owner and other than their own special function, they would also serve as a means of heaven–earth communication.

Last but not least, given the availability of quite advanced bronze casting technology, the fragility of wooden structural joints could be readily resolved by using bronze fittings. At the outset, the likelihood of developing a similar pictorial and typological vocabulary for structural joints through using another material, that is, wood, would not be substantial. At any rate, the development of bronze technology and art in early China had a seminal influence on architecture.

---

59 Chang, *Art, Myth, and Ritual*, 64–65.
60 Ibid., 45–47.

Chapter 2

THE DEVELOPMENT OF COLUMN AND BRACKET SETS IN THE HAN DYNASTY

Although wooden structures have dominated Chinese architecture for more than three millennia, none from before the Tang dynasty have survived. Fortunately, their forms were mirrored in stone architecture, reliefs, pottery models (*mingqi*), murals, and even decorative housewares. The Han dynasty, in particular, gave rise to numerous representations of *dougong* in tomb structures, stone reliefs, pottery models, freestanding stone towers (*que*), and literary descriptions. My research builds on these available sources.[1]

To Liang Sicheng and Liu Zhiping, the development of *dougong* in architecture reached mature status during the Han dynasty.[2] Yet they, like most modern researchers, have regarded it primarily as a structural element, and their analyses have been largely typological, tracing the evolution of various *dougong* systems over succeeding dynasties. As Nancy Steinhardt has summarized, "Han bracket sets were studied according to three principal features used in all later bracketing"— that is, the cap block and other blocks, the arm, and the number of layers.[3]

Chapter 2 takes a different approach, examining the column and bracket set not as a formal or structural element, but as a symbolic, social, and cultural one. In this respect, I partly follow the lead of Jiren Feng, who has studied the symbolic associations of column and bracket sets in the Song dynasty. Through a detailed analysis of literary sources from the tenth to the twelfth centuries, with the focus on *Yingzao fashi*, Feng points out that the multilayered *dougong* system was often likened to flowers and branches to suggest

---

1 Han tomb reliefs, in particular, have been widely dispersed, and it is often difficult to specify their original location and purpose. This study has benefitted greatly from the examples compiled in Li Guoxin and Yang Wenjing, eds, *Zhongguo Hanhua zaoxing yishu tudian-jianzhu* (Zhengzhou, 2014), hereby abbreviated as ZHZYT-J.

2 Liang Sicheng and Liu Zhiping, "Dougong jianshuo," in: *Liang Sicheng quanji* (Beijing, 2001), VI, 291.

3 Nancy S. Steinhardt, *Chinese Architecture in an Age of Turmoil, 200–600* (Honolulu, 2014), 83.

the auspicious "blossoming" of the structure.[4] Although Feng adduces some physical and literary evidence from early China to support his argument, I find that the meanings attendant on the column and bracket set in earlier centuries differed considerably from those prevalent during the Tang–Song dynasties. The account below focuses on the role of *dougong* during the Han dynasty, when the element was primarily associated not with natural forms, but rather with beliefs about the heavens, mythology, and the afterlife.

The Political Symbolism of the Han Dynasty

As the second regime to unify the central territories of what is now known as China, the Han dynasty is commonly regarded as a golden age in Chinese history, the influence of which is still evident. The Han gives its name, for example, to China's majority ethnic group and to its common written script. As a result of the brief interruption by the Xin dynasty (9–23), founded by the former Han regent Wang Mang 王莽 (45 BCE–23 CE), the Han dynasty was divided into two periods: the Western Han or Former Han (206 BCE–9 CE) and the Eastern Han or Later Han (25–220). Given the short duration of the first imperial dynasty, the Qin dynasty, the Han dynasty strove to achieve an enduring and unified empire.

The most significant achievement by the Han empire was to establish a cosmological basis for its rule, a unity between heaven, earth, and man. To this end, the Han court sponsored Confucianism in education and court politics. This aim is particularly evident in the *Chunqiu fanlu* 春秋繁露, compiled by Dong Zhongshu 董仲舒 (179–104 BCE), which promoted Confucianism as an official doctrine.[5] In addition, earlier beliefs such as astrology and *wuxing* 五行, the theory of Five Elements, were further developed in the Han dynasty to guide political life and to consolidate imperial sovereignty as the Mandate of Heaven. Astrological portents were followed closely by the ruler and high dignitaries and served to conduct major affairs of state.[6] In the court documents recording the history of the Han dynasty (e.g., *Hanshu* 汉书 and *Hou Hanshu* 后汉书), there are special volumes dedicated to astronomy and *wuxing* that accentuate a seamless fusion between politics and cosmology.[7] In a chapter about astronomy in *Shiji* 史记,

4 Jiren Feng, *Chinese Architecture and Metaphor: Song Culture in the Yingzao Fashi Building Manual* (Honolulu, 2012), 138–180.

5 Dong Zhongshu, *Chunqiu fanlu* (Zhengzhou, 2010).

6 David Pankenier, *Astrology and Cosmology in Early China: Conforming Earth to Heaven* (New York, 2013), 300.

7 Ban Gu, *Hanshu* (Xi'an, 2006); Fan Ye, *Hou Hanshu* (Xi'an, 2006).

Sima Qian司马迁 (c. 145–86 BCE) used the different titles of official positions in naming the constellations. The chapter is entitled "Tianguan shu" 天官书 (Treatise on the Celestial Offices), emphasizing the linkage between celestial stars and court officialdom.[8] Indeed, the Han dynasty saw a synthesis of cosmic patterns and political life, or, in Aihe Wang's words, oversaw a process of "moralising cosmology and transforming imperial sovereignty" that had a long-enduring influence on sociopolitical life in Imperial China.[9]

A concomitant desire to bring heavenly order to earth was common in architecture. The cosmic-magical symbolism of the Chinese city had existed since ancient times, although it was in the Han dynasty, as David Pankenier has demonstrated, that the layout of cities according to the observed pattern of the constellations became a codified tradition, reflected in both theory and practice.[10] Heavenly symbolism and ritual were especially pronounced in the audience hall of the Imperial Palace, or Bright Hall, where the emperor received and delivered his mandate to rule.[11] Even the construction of a royal carriage might be said to obey the laws of heaven. The rules were recorded by the Western Han scholar Jia Yi 贾谊 (200–168 BCE) in his political treatise *Xinshu* 新书:

> To make a carriage in ancient times, the canopy would be in a circular shape symbolising heaven, and there are twenty-eight ribs supporting the canopy that symbolise the twenty-eight constellations. The carriage in a square shape symbolises the earth. There are thirty spokes symbolising the moon [...].[12]

Many artifacts from early China, particularly those intended for imperial use, were bestowed with similar associations.

The rite of worship was not a passive process of admiring from a distance, but rather an active one that sought to link heaven and earth. As Lillian Lan-ying Tseng has argued, the search for immortality rose in popularity during the Han society, particularly among the upper classes.[13] Emperor Wu of Han 汉武帝 (156–87 BCE), for example, a gifted politician and military

8 Sima Qian, "Tianguan shu," in *Shiji* (Wuhan, 2017), vol. 1, 477–520.

9 Aihe Wang, *Cosmology and Political Culture in Early China* (Cambridge, 2000), 129–172.

10 See Pankenier, *Astrology and Cosmology in Early China*, 329–339, and Paul Wheatley, *The Origins and Character of the Ancient Chinese City*, 2 vols (Somerset, NJ, 2008).

11 See Lillian Lan-ying Tseng, *Picturing Heaven in Early China* (Cambridge, MA, 2011), 37–88.

12 Jia Yi, *Xinshu* (Beijing, 2012), 200–201.

13 Tseng, *Picturing Heaven in Early China*.

commander, devoted intensive efforts to deify himself.[14] It is possibly due to his influence that the literature portraying supernatural phenomena such as shamans, immortals, and mythical landscapes flourished in the Han dynasty.[15] Belief in the afterlife became widespread, which is evident in tomb art and architecture of the era. It is within the social context of longing for heaven that the production of columns and bracket sets will be considered.

The Earth and the Heavens

In early Chinese mythology, heaven and earth were separated by divine force, and this division was sustained by the pillars of heaven (天柱, *tianzhu*), that is, giant columns that supported the heavens and also served as a vertical connection with the earth. This symbolism appears in the two myths recorded in various literary sources from the Western Han period onward. One is about the god Pangu 盘古 who divided the heavens from the earth, with his body acting as a giant pillar.[16] The other myth regards the goddess Nüwa 女娲, who replaced the collapsing heavenly pillars with the four legs of a huge turtle.[17]

The pillars of heaven were manifest in Han arts and architecture. According to Wu Qingzhou, the Han column with two or three *dougong* above was understood to resemble an erect human body with two arms (and head) holding the structure above (Figure 2.1).[18] Wu further speculates about the analogy between the *dougong* system and a human skeleton, likening its multilayered components to those of a human spine. Although there is little evidence that columns were consciously shaped to resemble the human body in Han times, we do find anthropomorphic symbolism in cases of tomb architecture and ceramic models. A three-story pottery model of a pavilion from the late Eastern Han period, from Huaiyang County (Henan Province), employs human forms as columns (Figure 2.2). Exhibiting simultaneously male and female sexual organs, these beings may have held a certain religious or mythical status.

---

14 Sima, *Shiji*, vol. 1, chapter 12, 331–361.

15 See, for example, *Hanwu di bieguo dongming ji* by Guo Xian, and *Hanwu di neizhuan* and *Hanwu gushi* by anonymous Han writers. These myths are all collected in a single volume: *Xijing zaji (wai wu zhong)* (Shanghai, 2012).

16 Lü Simian, "Pangu kao," in *Zhongguo shenhua xue bainian wenlun xuan* (Xi'an, 2013), I, 252–255.

17 Lü Simian, "Nüwa yu Gonggong," in *Zhongguo shenhua xue bainian wenlun xuan*, 246–251.

18 Wu Qingzhou, *Jianzhu zheli, yijiang yu wenhua* (Beijing, 2005), 26–27.

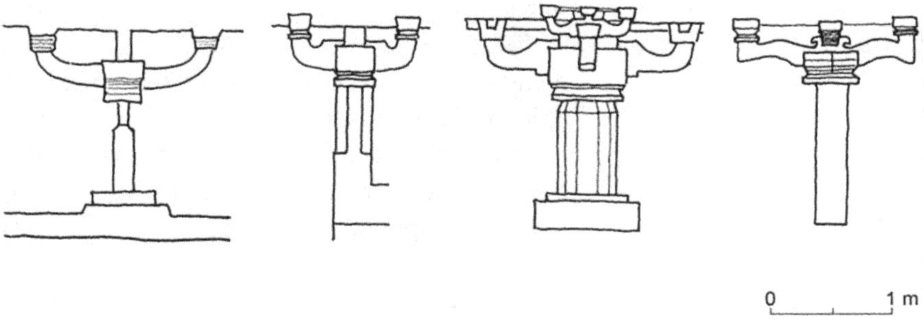

Figure 2.1 Columns from Han tombs unearthed in Sichuan Province (author's drawing, based on *Kaogu*, 1 (2002), figs 23, 27, 29 and 45).

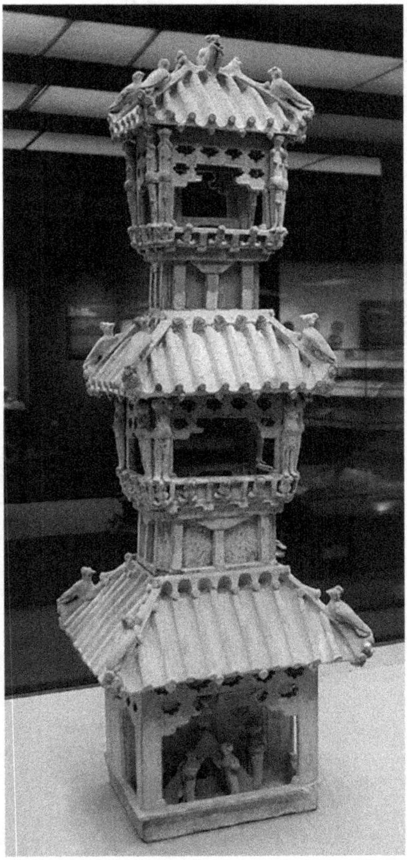

Figure 2.2 Three-story pottery pavilion from the later Eastern Han dynasty, unearthed at Jiunuzhong village, Huaiyang County, Henan Province (Henan Museum, author's photo, 2021).

The book *Shenyi jing* 神异经, attributed to Dongfang Shuo 东方朔 (c. 160–93 BCE), states that "there is a bronze pillar on the Kunlun Mountain, high enough to reach heaven, therefore it is called 'the heavenly pillar'."[19] In a Han bronze mirror dating from 25 to 220, discovered in Shaoxing, Zhejiang Province, a pillar is guarded by a huge animal tied to it by a chain (Figure 2.3). Set in a series of concentric rings beginning with the outer or earthly realm, the pillar appears as if supporting the inner, celestial world. The inscription to its right clearly names the pillar as *tongzhu* 铜柱 (bronze pillar). The bronze pillar was widely understood to represent an architectural connection to heaven. In the Later Han book *Hanwu gushi* 汉武故事, for example, a shaman suggested to the emperor that gods desired quietness, so the emperor built a great hall named "Shenming dian" 神明殿 (Hall of Divinities) outside the palace compound. The columns of the hall were made of bronze and even gilded.[20]

Literary sources also speak of bronze columns in palace buildings. The book *Yan Dan zi* 燕丹子, the Han version of the famous story about Jing Ke 荆轲, a retainer of Crown Prince Dan of the Yan state (1044–222 BCE), describes his

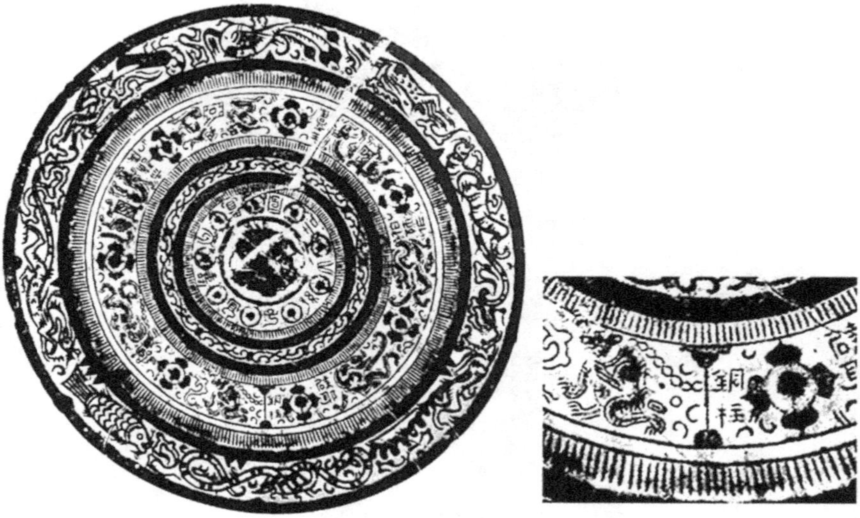

Figure 2.3 Rubbing from a Han bronze mirror, unearthed at Shaoxing, Zhejiang Province, showing a concentric pattern with celestial creatures and a column (Wang Shilun, ed., *Zhejiang chutu tongjing xuanji* (Beijing, 2006), fig. 20).

19 Dongfang Shuo, *Shenyi jing*, in *Bowu zhi* (*wai qi zhong*), 98.

20 *Hanwu gushi*, in *Xijing zaji* (*wai wu zhong*), 97–98.

failed assassination attempt against the ruler of the Qin state. The plan was conceived with the noble intention of saving the other six major states from annihilation by the Qin army. The attempt took place in the great hall of the Qin palace compound. Jing Ke threw his dagger at the Qin king, but he dodged the knife and it hit the bronze column, producing sparks.[21] Although Jing Ke was executed for his offence, he was regarded by later generations as a righteous man, given that the reign of the Qin king (who later became the first emperor) was commonly viewed as a crude tyranny. This story was also popularly reflected in stone reliefs from Han tombs that represent Jing Ke as immortal.[22] In the Wu Family Shrine 武氏祠, for example, an Eastern Han tomb in Jiaxiang County (Shandong Province, built in the second century), a stone relief carving vividly depicted the story of Jing Ke's assassination attempt in its middle portion.[23] Unlike the bronze column briefly mentioned in *Yan Dan zi*, the bronze column in the relief becomes the central element organizing the narrative (Figure 2.4). Consistent with the transformation of Jing Ke from a heroic assassin to a deity, the column, surmounted by a cap block (*dou*) and a miniature roof, is a free-standing form pointing to the sky, suggesting a vertical transformation from earth to heaven. More substantial and costly than a wooden column, a bronze column seemed a fitting metaphor for the heavenly pillar and was exclusively adopted in the royal palace buildings and major temples.

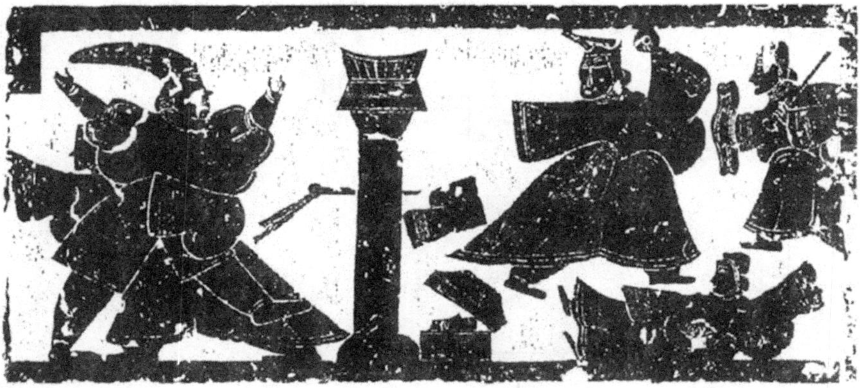

Figure 2.4 Rubbing of a stone relief from the Wu Family Shrine, an Eastern Han tomb unearthed in Jiaxiang County, Shandong Province (see Zhu Xilu, ed., *Wushi ci Han huaxiang shi* (Jinan, 1986), 51, fig. 49).

21 *Yan Dan zi*, in *Bowu zhi (wai qi zhong)*, 84.

22 Jiang Sheng, "Handai liexian tukao," *Journal of Chinese Humanities*, 2 (2015), 24.

23 For detailed study on Wu Family Shrine, please see Wu Hung, *The Wu Liang Shrine: The Ideology of Early Chinese Pictorial Art* (Stanford, 1989).

The longing to ascend to heaven is perhaps more explicitly reflected in tomb architecture.[24] Indeed, burial chambers were the most fitting place for such architectural symbolism. To illustrate the lofty and unattainable nature of heaven, both pillars and "gates of heaven" were employed. As a funerary motif, they blossomed in the Han period and stimulated a wide variety of artistic endeavors over the centuries.[25] In the Han tomb (48 BCE–8 CE) excavated in 1957 in Luoyang, architectural and pictorial depictions of the gate of heaven are evident.[26] In the center of the main chamber, a stone column supports a painted gable (Figure 2.5). One side of the gable, facing the rear chamber and the remains of the tomb owners, shows a gate with a narrow opening between two door planks. The portal is guarded by two winged dragons with riders (Figure 2.6), which apparently served to escort the deceased through the gate to heaven. Note the iconographic role of the stone column, which both supports the gate of heaven and connects the tomb to the celestial world.

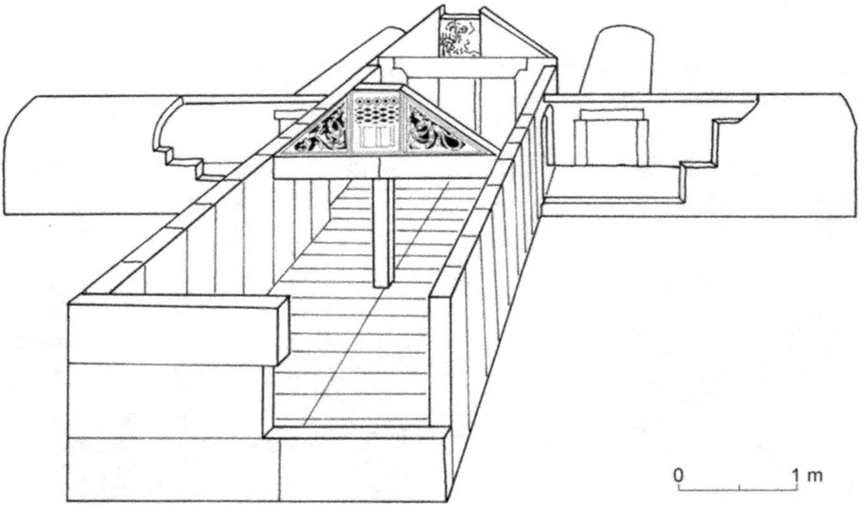

Figure 2.5 A perspective drawing (from west to east) of the Han tomb unearthed in Luoyang, Henan Province (author's drawing, based on *Kaogu xuebao*, 2 (1964), 110, fig. 2).

24 For details, see Wu Hung, *The Art of the Yellow Springs: Understanding Chinese Tombs* (London, 2010).

25 Tseng, *Picturing Heaven in Early China*, 205.

26 The Archaeological Team from Bureau of Culture in Henan Province, "Luoyang Xihan bihuamu fajue baogao," *Kaogu xuebao*, 2 (1964), 107–126.

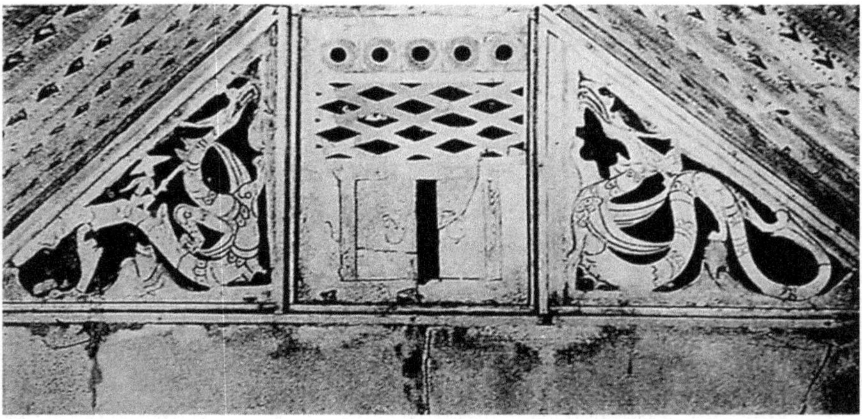

Figure 2.6 Painted gable above the stone column in the Han tomb, Luoyang, Henan Province (*Kaogu xuebao*, 2 (1964), 110, fig. 3).

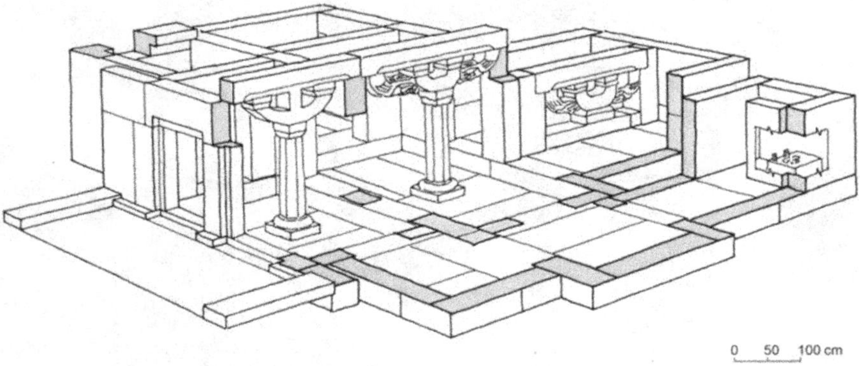

Figure 2.7 An axonometric drawing of the Beizhai tomb unearthed in Yi'nan County, Shandong Province (author's drawing, based on *Yi'nan guhuaxiang shimu fajue baogao*, 4, fig. 3).

In another Han tomb from the late second century, unearthed in Beizhai village, Yi'nan County (Shandong Province), octagonal stone columns and bracket sets were placed centrally in the two main chambers (Figure 2.7).[27] According to Steinhardt's research on Han architecture, the octagonal

27 For details, see Nanjing Museum and Cultural Relics Management Office of Shandong Province, *Yi'nan guhuaxiang shimu fajue baogao* (Beijing, 1956); Lydia Thompson, *The Yi'nan Tomb: Narrative and Ritual in Pictorial Art of the Eastern Han (25–220 CE.)* (New York University, 1998).

shape is found in tomb plans, ceiling configurations, and pillars of heaven. The octagon reflected the Chinese symbol for the number eight and also served as a cosmological diagram referring to the directions and winds.[28] The column system in the central chamber divides it into eastern and western halves. The column cap block supports the bracket set above, which in turn holds the massive central rib of the ceiling (Figure 2.8). The heads of two carved dragons extend the bracket set, thereby reinforcing the structural support of the column. Represented as celestial creatures, the dragons appear to descend from the sky, as though trailing their serpentine bodies above the plane of the ceiling.

The whole column structure in the Beizhai tomb abounds with celestial motifs. The western sides of the column shaft are incised with mythical figures and flying animals, such as winged dragons, *qilin*, birds, winged turtles, and the Queen Mother of the West (Xiwangmu, Figure 2.9). As a popular

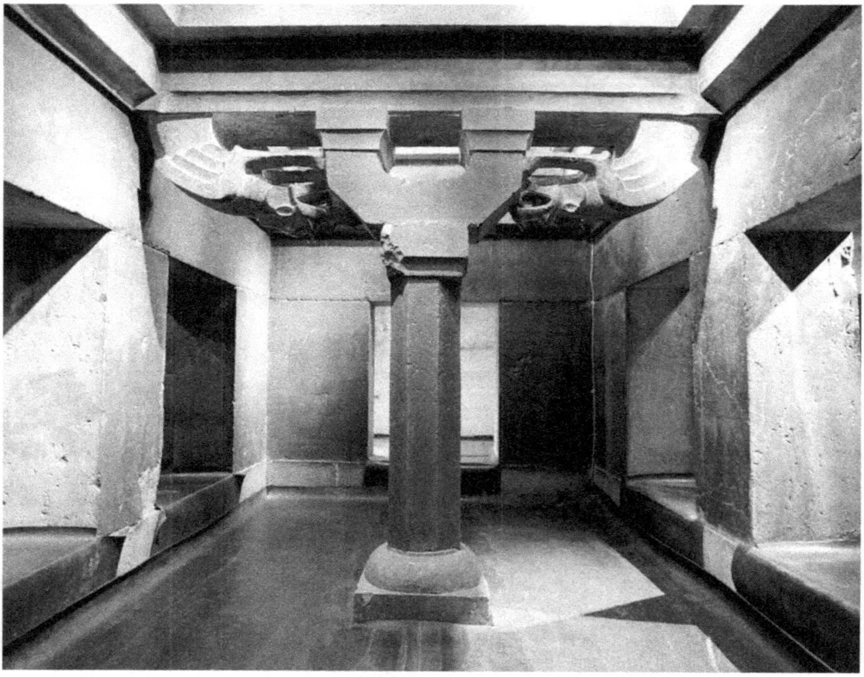

Figure 2.8 The pillar of heaven in the central chamber of the Beizhai tomb, Yi'nan County, Shandong Province (author's photo, 2022).

28 Steinhardt, *Chinese Architecture in an Age of Turmoil*, 93.

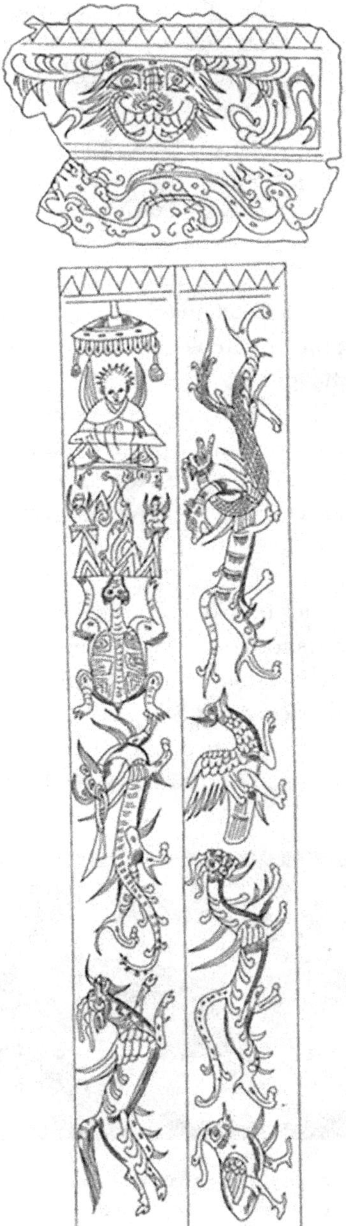

Figure 2.9 Redrawing of the carved motifs on the cap block and two western sides of the pillar of heaven in the Beizhai tomb, Yi'nan County, Shandong Province (Shandong Museum, ed., *Yi'nan Beizhai Hanmu huaxiang* (Beijing, 2015), 83, fig. 55).

goddess in the Han dynasty, the Queen Mother was believed to be in charge of the land of the immortals near, on or above Kunlun Mountain.[29] In this architectural representation of the column, the Queen Mother of the West is placed at the very top of the shaft facing west. She is enshrined by a decorative canopy and sits above a mountain whose shape resembles the Chinese character of a mountain (山, *shan*). Held up by a winged turtle, this mountain with three peaks clearly represents Kunlun Mountain. The cap block above the column is engraved with the head of a horned beast atop a swirling cloud pattern. A similar swirling cloud motif also appears on the two blocks above the bracket arm (Figure 2.10). In view of the prevalence of these celestial motifs, the archaeologists named the two octagonal columns *Qingtian zhu* 擎天柱 (the pillars of heaven) in their excavation report of the tomb published in 1956. Lydia Thompson, in her PhD dissertation, further points out that the two pillars transform the tomb into a sacred center linking Heaven and Earth, embodying a single *axis mundi*.[30] In comparison with other Han tomb structures and iconic decorations, Wu Hung confirms that the Yi'nan pillar "would enable the tomb occupant, or his soul, to reach the immortal abode after his demise."[31]

The stone column and bracket set in the Beizhai tomb most likely imitated wooden examples found in elite domestic architecture at that time. Among many earthly scenes found in the relief sculptures in the Beizhai tomb, the central chamber contains a depiction of a large rectangular house consisting of two courtyards (Figure 2.11). The front court contains a well, indicated by the presence of a windlass. The back court features a long table

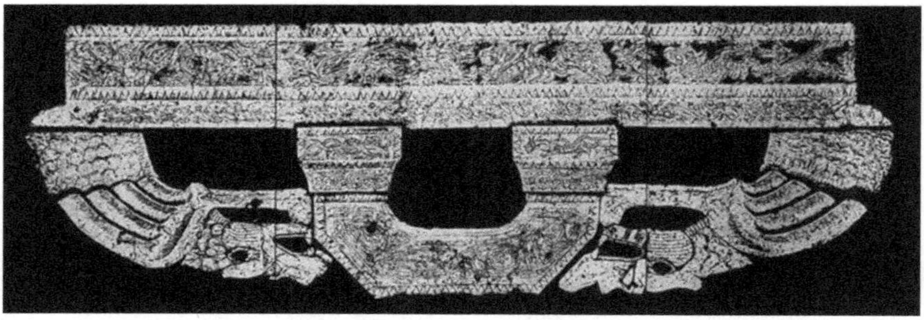

Figure 2.10 Rubbing of the bracket set from the pillar of heaven in the Beizhai tomb, Yi'nan County, Shandong Province (*Yi'nan guhuaxiang shimu fajue baogao*, plate 75).

29 Tseng, *Picturing Heaven in Early China*, 261.
30 Thompson, *The Yi'nan Tomb*, 157.
31 Wu Hung, *The Art of the Yellow Springs*, 57.

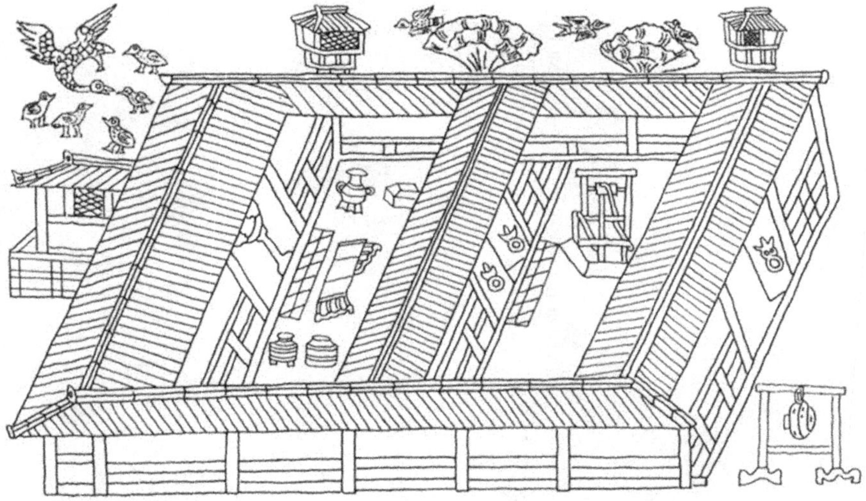

Figure 2.11 Courtyard house from a stone relief in the Beizhai tomb, Yi'nan County, Shandong Province (author's drawing, based on *Yi'nan guhuaxiang shimu fajue baogao*, plate 103, fig. 1).

in the center flanked by urns. The front court appears to be dedicated to daily life and the back court to formal ritual activity. A column with a curved bracket set stands at the threshold of the central room facing the back court. The importance of this column, with its similar configuration to the pillars of heaven in the tomb, is underlined by its central location and its distinctive form. Considering the uniqueness of the column and bracket set and their loose connection to the house structure, Han Baode speculates that it must have conveyed some form of religious meaning, although he was unable to elaborate on his point.[32] Similar columns with arched bracket sets also repeatedly appear in stone reliefs from the same tomb. In these carved representations, the column separates the opening into halves, spatially and visually establishing its central position (see Figure 2.12).

In his inquiry about the origin of *dougong*, Yang Hongxun points out that there was a physical transformation of the bracket set, in particular the bracket arm, in early China—from a square form (欂, *bo*) to a curved form (栾, *luan*), with the latter widespread in the Han period. Yang further claims that *luan* (curved bracket arm) was often decorated with a dragon pattern or,

32 Han Baode, *Ming-Qing Jianzhu er'lun/Dougong de qiyuan yu fazhan* (Beijing, 2014), 117.

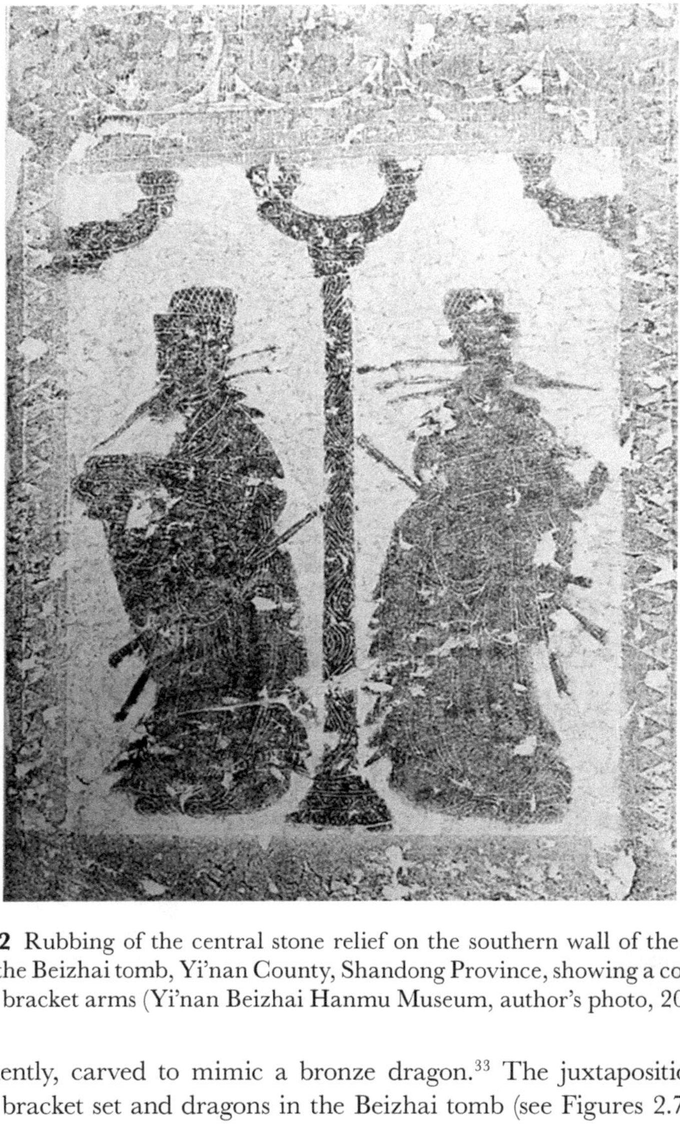

Figure 2.12 Rubbing of the central stone relief on the southern wall of the front chamber in the Beizhai tomb, Yi'nan County, Shandong Province, showing a column with curved bracket arms (Yi'nan Beizhai Hanmu Museum, author's photo, 2022).

more frequently, carved to mimic a bronze dragon.[33] The juxtaposition of the curved bracket set and dragons in the Beizhai tomb (see Figures 2.7 and 2.8) seems to verify Yang's point.

Evidence for the ritual importance of *dougong* also exists in aboveground structures. *Que*, free-standing ceremonial towers, were analogous to tombs in the Han period as bearers of a transcendent architectural symbolism.

33 Yang Hongxun, "Dougong qiyuan kaocha," in: *Jianzhu kaoguxue lunwenji* (Beijing, 1987), 260–261.

As can be seen from extant examples and pertinent images in stone reliefs, they consisted of a large pavilion-like structure set atop a series of bracket sets, the whole supported by a wide shaft (Figures 2.13 and 2.14). Most remaining Han *que* are stone structures, although they must also have existed in wood. As summarized by Chen Mingda, wooden Han *que* consisted of columns topped with square battens arranged in a crisscross pattern,

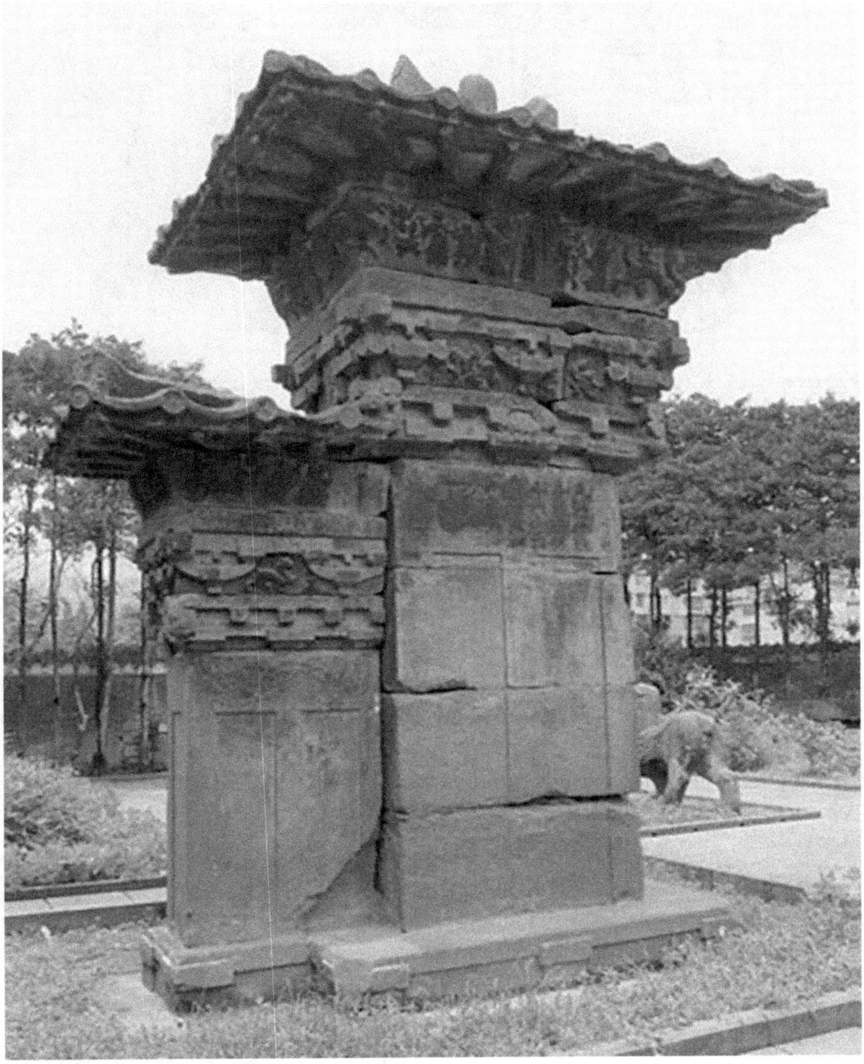

Figure 2.13 Gaoyi Que, the Han *que* in Ya'an, Sichuan Province (photograph by Zeus1234, Wikimedia Commons).

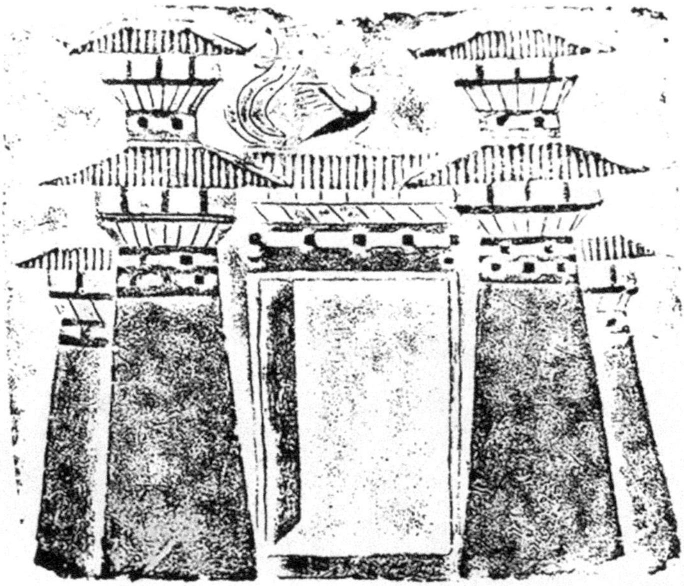

Figure 2.14 Que depicted in a rubbing from a Han brick relief unearthed in Dayi County, Sichuan Province (ZHZYT-J, 235, fig. 1).

terminating in bracket sets—a logical solution for building atop the tall shaft.[34] Although the stone bracket sets in Han *que* serve as decorative rather than structural elements, their physical details are truthfully presented, and they offer a valuable subject for modern studies of *dougong* in early Chinese architecture.

As a part of palace building, the origin of *que* can be traced back to the Zhou dynasty (1046–256 BCE), but their development as a ceremonial gateway for tombs, palaces, and temples reached its peak during the Han dynasty. Song Yanping has illustrated the functional transformation of *que* during this period.[35] Early *que* in the pre-Qin dynasty (before 221 BCE) were symbols of authority. For example, *que* were used to display legal provisions. As tall structures, *que* also served as lookouts—possibly for military observation as well as watching parades. According to Song's detailed study, it was during the Han dynasty that the functions of *que* became mystical and ritualized as a heavenly "gate" through which immortality could be acquired.[36] This transformation mirrors the development of architecture

34 Chen Mingda, *Zhongguo gudai mujiegou jianzhu jishu: Zhanguo-Beisong* (Beijing, 1990), 31.

35 Song Yanping, "Cong 'que' dao 'tianmen'—Han que de shenmihua lichen," *Sichuan Cultural Relics*, 5 (2016), 60–68.

36 Ibid.

in the Han dynasty and underlines the period's tendency toward cosmological symbolism. Like the pillar of heaven, two *que* (or two clusters of *que*) were often placed in a pair forming a gateway for important tombs, palaces, and temples, serving as a religious or symbolic link to heaven. This practice was echoed by the Han book *Shenyi jing*:

> There are two golden *que* in the Northwest Wasteland. Their height is one hundred *zhang* [about 330 metres ...] and so is the distance between them. [...] There is a flight of golden stairs running from the northwest and passing between these two *que*, which is called *tianmen* 天门 [the gate of heaven].[37]

Vividly depicted in many reliefs from the Han period, the gate of heaven was formed by a pair of *que* as gate posts symmetrically articulating a threshold. In addition, the Chinese words "*tianmen*" also appear in the middle of two *que* in some bronze vessels and stone reliefs denoting the theme of the gate of heaven (Figures 2.15 and 2.16).

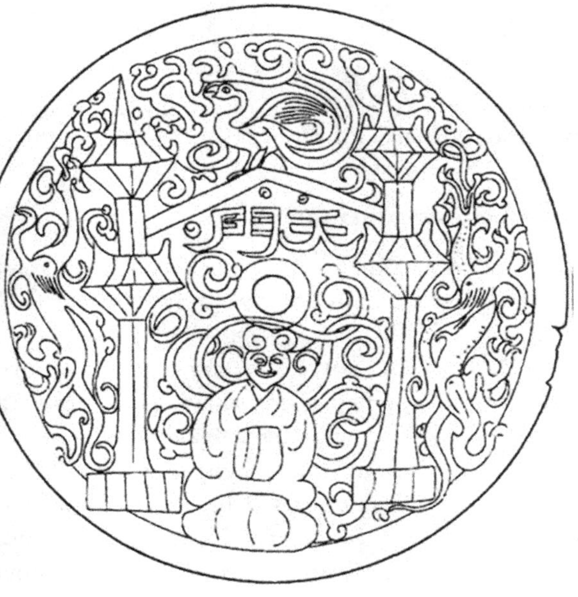

Figure 2.15 The gate of heaven formed by que, redrawn from a Han bronze vessel unearthed in Wushan County, Chongqing (ZHZYT-J, 260, fig. 1).

---

37 Dongfang, *Shenyi jing*, in *Bowu zhi (wai qi zhong)*, 97.

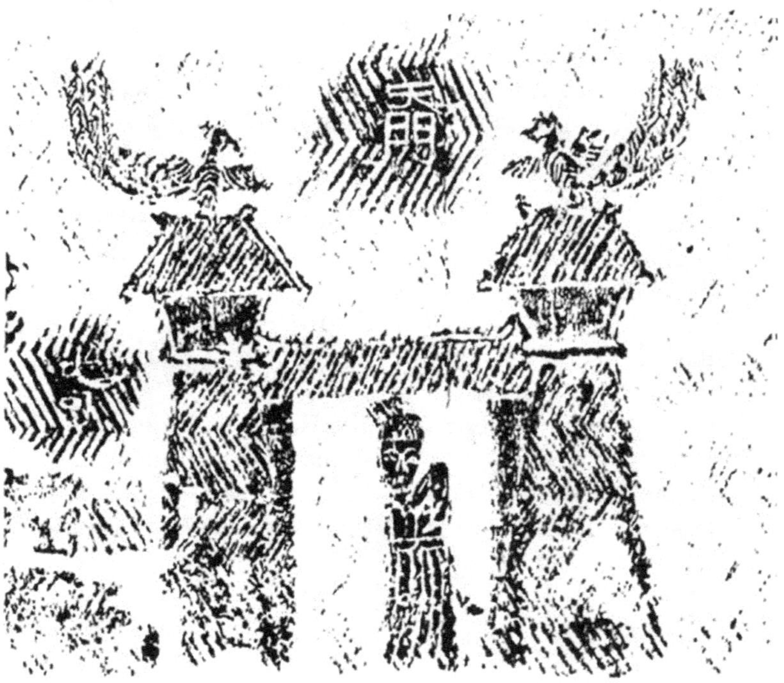

Figure 2.16 The gate of heaven formed by que, from a rubbing of a Han stone relief unearthed in Jianyang, Sichuan Province (ZHZYT-J, 270, fig. 2).

The Stars and Constellations

The literature of the Han period also confirms that architecture, particularly that of great halls, embodies heavenly order. The Hall of Numinous Brilliance (灵光殿, Lingguang dian), for example, built at Qufu (now Shandong Province) in the Western Han period and surviving well into the Eastern Han period, was described as having been constructed according to cosmic patterns. Reflecting upon the longevity of the hall, Wang Yanshou 王延寿 (c. 140–165), an Eastern Han scholar, declared: "I wonder if this could be because a divine intelligence rested here and supported it to preserve the Han house. Yet, that its design and dimensions correspond to the stars and constellations above is further reason for its prolonged stability."[38]

38 Wang Yanshou, "*Lu Lingguang dian fu*," in: *Zhaoming Wen Xuan* (Beijing, 2000), 324–335. The English translation is by David Knechtges in *Wen Xuan or Selections of Refined Literature, Volume II: Rhapsodies on Sacrifices, Hunting, Travel, Sightseeing, Palaces and Halls, Rivers and Seas* (Princeton, NJ, 1983), 263.

Wang was not a craftsman and may not have understood building techniques very well. However, as a well-known tradition in Imperial China, it was often the literati's reading of a building and its conceptualization through text that established its broader cultural meaning.[39]

In his *Lu Lingguang dian fu* 鲁灵光殿赋, Wang Yanshou portrayed the architecture of the hall in detail:

> We carefully examine ridgepole and roof,
> View its manner of construction.
> The design corresponds to the heavens,
> Above, is modeled on the Loggerhead [a constellation].
> [...]
> Floating posts, sublimely soaring, suspended like stars,
> are perilously poised on high, cleaving and clinging.
> Flying rafters, arched and arced, pointing like rainbows.
> raised aloft, great and grand, soar *en masse.*[40]

Although not specified as bracket sets, Wang identified the structural elements, such as the floating posts and flying rafters, as "stars" and "rainbows." Similar metaphors can be found in *Jingfu dian fu* 景福殿赋 by He Yan 何晏 (?–249). This palace hall was built sometime after 232 in the Wei city of Xuchang. The author portrayed the interior space as dark and gloomy, cloaked by the curtain of night, against which the upper structural elements would shine like stars:

> Its inner recesses:
> Shrouded and veiled, dark and dim,
> vague visions, fading forms,
> are like night stars continuously conjoined.
> [...]
> Now for its construction:
> Long beams, colorfully designed,
> Straddle openings below, rest wondrously poised above.
> Purlins and struts, manifoldly layered,
> their strength engaged, their forms disjoined.

39 For a detailed discussion of the conceptualisation of architecture in imperial China, see Jing Xie, "Transcending the Limitations of Physical Form: A Case Study of Cang Lang Pavilion," *Journal of Architecture*, 21.5 (2016), 691–718.

40 Knechtges, *Wen Xuan or Selections of Refined Literature, Volume II*, 269.

Scarlet as arching rainbows,
red as dashing wiverns.
South reach the sunlit eaves [*yangrong*, southern eave],
North extend to the darkest limits [*youya*, northern boundary].
Though their load is heavy, and their course long,
Their service is exceedingly great.[41]

Here the multilayered bracket sets are termed purlins (桁, *hang*) and struts (梧, *wu*), their forms likened to rainbows and wyverns. As the above account describes it, the southern edge of the hall was bright. The term *yangrong* 阳荣 was later used specifically to refer in architectural terminology to the "southern eave." By contrast, the northern side was dark and concealed. Such usage suggests that Chinese houses were laid out on a north–south axis to take advantage of the morning light (Figure 2.17). The brightest spot was the open courtyard, followed by an intermediate zone of the veranda covered by the southern eave, and eventually the darkest area at the internal northern boundary. Such a layout was aligned with the court etiquette for conducting the morning audience.

As recorded in the early Confucian lexicon *Erya* 尔雅, arguably completed in the early Western Han period, there was a rigid order for positioning the ruler and his audiences in the courtyard of a ruler's house. Under the southern eave of the great hall was a veranda where the ruler would stand facing south, that is, in the courtyard. This was the place that distinguished

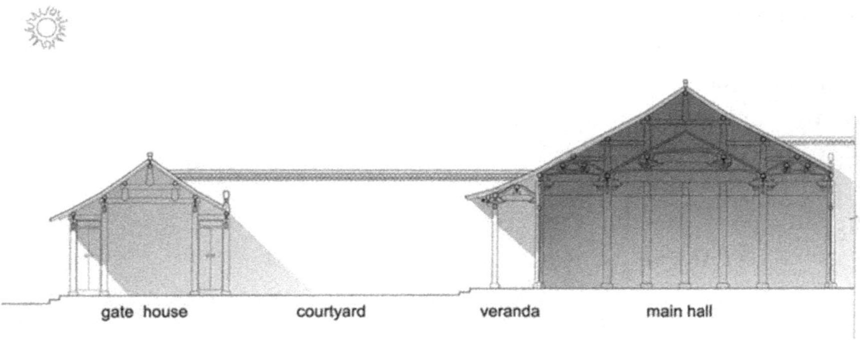

Figure 2.17 Shadow diagram of the cross section of a typical courtyard house (author's drawing).

41 He Yan, "*Jingfu dian fu*," in: *Zhaoming Wen Xuan*, 336–353. The English translation is by Knechtges, *Wen Xuan or Selections of Refined Literature, Volume II*, 285 and 287.

the ruler from the officials, and it was called *xiang* 乡 (native place). If this place was bright, then the world would be governed in an orderly way. In the courtyard, there were left and right sides called *wei* 位 (position), with designated locations for each official to conduct court audiences.[42] The veranda, under which a ruler stood, was often emphasized by inserting an extra roof layer, forming a double-eave roof. Such architectural accents had long existed for great halls since the late Western Zhou period.

He Yan's description of the great hall's darkness is also apt. As both archaeological and literary sources indicate, the great hall in its early form contained private sleeping chambers.[43] In contrast to the court business to be conducted in the light near the opening of the hall, the interior was to be dark and secluded to enhance privacy. As He suggests, it offered a mystical space where human imagination soared: "vague visions, fading forms, are like night stars."

The Han analogy between bracket set and the constellations was still valid in the Song dynasty. When the rebuilding of the Jinci 晋祠 temple was completed in 984, the scholar Zhao Changyan 赵昌言 (944–1009) wrote an essay eulogizing the Song emperor's conquest and the architecture of Jinci. Zhao praised the great hall in particular: "the myriad brackets gather like constellations, a thousand pillars shimmer like seaweed."[44] It was traditional to paint the upper structural components with seaweed motifs as a way of warding off fire. Zhao's metaphor brings the otherworldliness of the hall to life by juxtaposing the realm of the sky with that of the oceans.

The star-like impression of bracket sets and upper structural elements was not only evident in literary sources but also in the connection between the Chinese character *dou* and its original pictography. Figure 2.18 shows the oracle bone inscription character for *dou*, meaning ladle, peck-measure, or dipper, which clearly resembles a ladle and refers in some contexts to the Northern Dipper (or the Southern Dipper).[45] Liu Xujie, in his research on the typology and evolution of *dougong* in the Han dynasty, discerns that the pictorial representation of *gong* (the bracket arm) evolved into various forms, while that of *dou* (block) consistently remained square or wedge shaped.[46] The integrity of *dou*

---

42 *Erya yizhu* (Shanghai, 2012), 210.

43 Some royal palaces from the Zhou dynasty had one main hall containing several chambers for private living. See Du Jinpeng, "Zhouyuan gongdian jianzhu leixing ji xiangguan wenti tantao," *Kaogu xuebao*, 4 (2009), 435–468.

44 Cited and translated in Tracy Miller, *The Divine Nature of Power: Chinese Ritual Architecture at the Sacred Site of Jinci* (Cambridge, MA, 2007), 68. I have slightly modified Miller's translation.

45 See the similar remarks in Pankenier, *Astrology and Cosmology in Early China*, 104.

46 Liu Xujie, "Handai dougong de leixing yu yanbian chutan," *Wenwu ziliao congkan*, 2 (1978), 222–228.

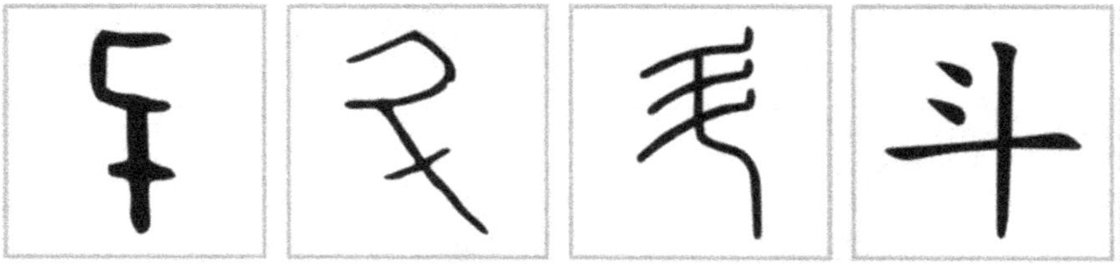

Figure 2.18 The transformation of the character *dou* 斗, from left to right: oracle bone inscription; bronze inscription; small seal script; regular script, *Han Dian*, zdic.net/z/1b/zy/6597.htm (accessed April 21, 2017).

was not only a result of its structural importance, but also, most likely, due to its fixed celestial connotation. Referring to the Northern Dipper, *dou* played an important role in astronomy for formulating the lunar calendar. In "Tianguan shu," Sima Qian wrote:

> The *dou* is the carriage of *di* [the supreme deity], operating in the centre while managing the four quarters. The *dou* also plays a crucial role for dividing *yin* and *yang*, establishing four seasons, balancing *wuxing* [the Five Elements], determining the shifting degree of the sun and seasons, and articulating the calendar.[47]

The significance of the Northern Dipper was vividly recorded in a stone carving in the Wu Family Shrine built in the second century (Figure 2.19). The supreme deity *di* is sitting in the scoop of a dipper formed by seven linked circles representing the seven stars of the constellation.

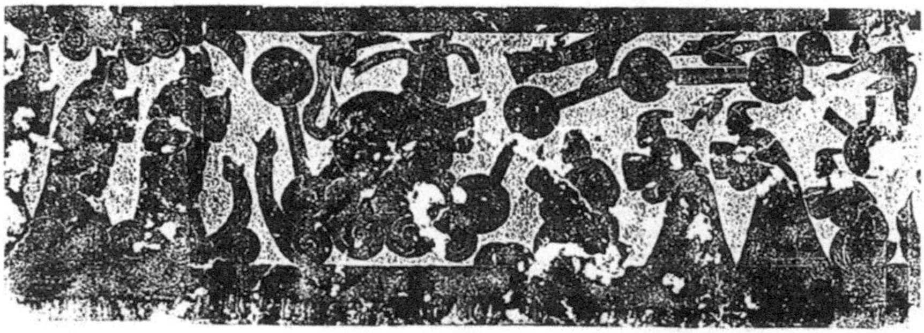

Figure 2.19 Rubbing of a stone relief from the Wu Family Shrine, an Eastern Han tomb unearthed in Jiaxiang County, Shandong Province (*Wushi ci Han huaxiang shi*, 40, fig. 35).

47 Sima, "Tianguan shu," in: *Shiji*, vol. 1, 478.

He is receiving his audience, which consists of four figures dressed like Han officials bowing and kneeling before him. Here we see a confluence in the symbolism of the Northern Dipper as both a celestial carriage and an architectural support of the firmament itself. It was only later that the word *dou* migrated to architectural terminology. In the Han lexicon *Shiming*, written between the late second and early third centuries, *dou* appears in the category of terms about housing: "*dou* is at the two ends of *luan* [that is, curved bracket arm], its shape is like a ladle; *dou* bears the weight from the above and stabilises [the structure]."[48]

The Holy Mountain

The earliest textual record of the bracket set is in *Lunyu* 论语 (*Analects*), compiled by Confucius's followers during the Warring States period and reaching its final form during the mid-Han dynasty. "*Shanjie zaozhuo*" 山节藻棁 is how Confucius (551–479 BCE) metaphorically described the upper structural components of a grand house.[49] *Shanjie* indicates that the bracket set resembles the shape of a mountain, while *zaozhuo* means the short post above the beam, which is decorated with seaweed motifs. The relationship between bracket set and mountain was not arbitrary. In early civilizations, mountains are often associated with divinity, and this was particularly true during the Han period. Driven by the imperial court's pursuit of immortality, the legendary Kunlun Mountain frequently appeared in the literature of this time. With its upper portion piercing the heavens, it was associated with immortal activity and often portrayed as the residence of the goddess Queen Mother of the West. Kunlun Mountain was far different in form to an ordinary mountain. Imagining the top as a capacious space for celestial landscapes, the literature of the period often depicted Kunlun Mountain as mushroom-shaped, wide at the top and narrow at the base. *Hainei shizhou ji* 海内十洲记, a book compiled between the third and fifth centuries, describes a triangle, or an upside-down pyramid, floating above Kunlun Mountain:

> There is a triangle above [Kunlun Mountain]. [Its top] is a squared area of one thousand *li*, its shape is like a basin [in elevation] which is narrow at the bottom and broad on the top, so it is called the Triangle of Kunlun Mountain.[50]

---

48 Liu Xi, *Shiming* (Beijing, 2016), 80.
49 *Lunyu* (Beijing, 2015), 64.
50 *Hainei shizhou ji*, in *Bowu zhi* (*wai qi zhong*) (Shanghai, 2012), 109.

The text further describes the four corners comprising the base of this "triangle," three of them facing the three cardinal points (i.e., north, west, and east) and the remaining one containing a celestial city with various buildings.[51] In addition, the text mentions other mountains on top of Kunlun Mountain, among which countless celestial palaces are built.[52]

Wu Hung also confirms that the mushroom-like summit on which Queen Mother of the West resides (which frequently appears in Han pictorial arts) depicts Kunlun Mountain.[53] The pictorial representations of the mountain are, however, diverse. As mentioned above, the relief on the octagonal column in the Beizhai tomb employs a figure with three peaks, representing the Chinese character of "mountain," to depict Kunlun Mountain (see Figure 2.9). Another relief from the same tomb depicts the Queen Mother of the West sitting atop the three peaks of the mountain, here transformed into three broad-topped pillars, their bases connected (Figure 2.20). The latter iconographic feature of Kunlun Mountain, as Wu Hung points out, is a combination of the mushroom-shaped mountain and the three-peaked structure.[54]

In addition, literary sources describe the landscape above Kunlun Mountain as having different layers. As recorded in *Huainan zi* 淮南子, compiled in the Western Han period sometime before 139 BCE, there are three layers above Kunlun Mountain:

> Ascending a height equal to Kunlun Mountain, above it there is the Mountain of Chill Wind. The climb up this mountain could make people immortal. Further climbing up an equal height, there is the Suspended Garden. Ascending here, one would obtain numinous power to summon wind and call for rain. Further climbing up an equal height, one would reach the sphere of heaven thereby becoming a god. This is the place where the Celestial Emperor lives.[55]

The physical depiction of the Kunlun Mountain and the celestial structures above it often took familiar architectural form. For example, many Eastern Han stone reliefs from Suide (Shaanxi Province) employ the motif of a giant pillar

---

51 Ibid., 109–110.

52 Ibid.

53 Wu Hung, "Xiwangmu, the Queen Mother of the West," *Orientations*, 18.4 (April 1987), 24–33.

54 Wu Hung, *The Wu Liang Shrine*, 119.

55 Liu An et al., *Huainan zi* (Beijing, 2014), 100.

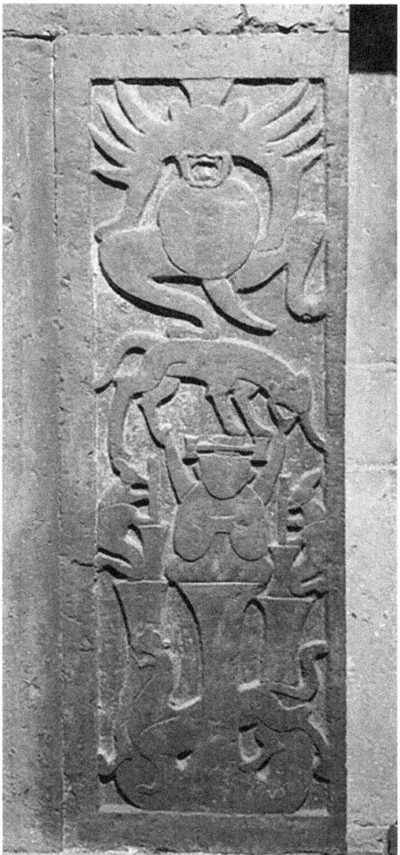

Figure 2.20 A stone relief of the Queen Mother of the West and Kunlun Mountain in the Beizhai tomb, Yi'nan County, Shandong Province (author's photo, 2022).

with layers of bracket sets above (Figure 2.21). From the mushroom-like shape of the bracket sets and the column cap, we see a clear analogy between the column and Kunlun Mountain, and another between the bracket sets and the celestial structures above Kunlun Mountain. In all these stone reliefs, exactly three layers of bracket sets rise above the column, most likely confirming the three layers above Kunlun Mountain mentioned in the literature. Yet the number of the layers could sometimes increase. For example, in *Shiyi ji* 拾遗记, compiled during the Jin dynasty (265–420), Kunlun Mountain contains nine layers and there is a distance of ten thousand *li* between each layer.[56]

56 Wang Jia, *Shiyi ji* (Beijing, 1988), 221.

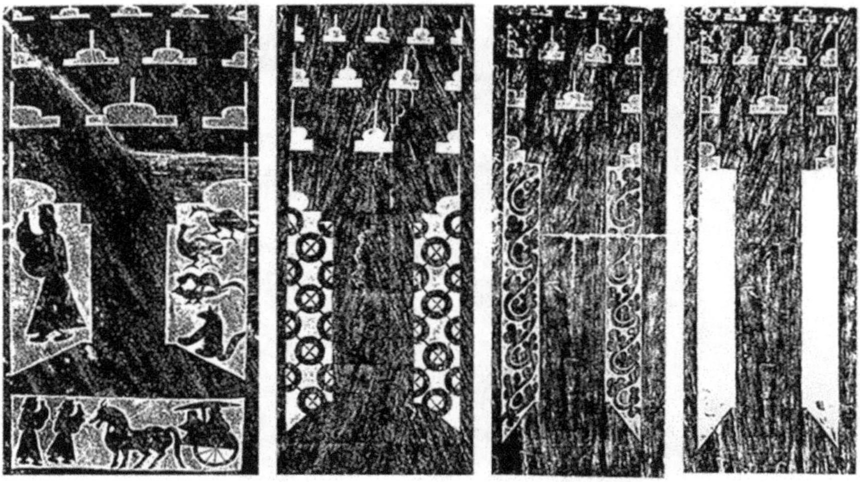

Figure 2.21 Rubbings of Eastern Han stone relief wall panels from a tomb in Suide County, Shaanxi Province, showing column and bracket sets (ZHZYT-J, 272, figs 1 and 2; 274, figs 2 and 3).

The stone reliefs depicting the giant columns originally formed vertical wall panels or decorated a freestanding column within a tomb. Connoting Kunlun Mountain, the giant column represented both the pillar of heaven and Kunlun Mountain, leading the deceased to ascend the upper structures above it. The same inverted-triangle form also served in more mundane contexts to represent the bracket set itself, as is noticeable in many stone reliefs and pottery models from the Han dynasty (Figures 2.22 and 2.23).

Landscape and Flora

The fantasy of immortality was also manifest in the written descriptions of celestial landscapes that prevailed in literature from the Han to the Jin dynasties. Celestial architecture required various giant and mythical trees as raw material, and examples of such appear in many texts such as *Shanhai jing* 山海经 and *Shenyi jing* 神异经 as well as carved reliefs as seen above in Figure 2.24.[57] With their innate upward growth, trees themselves served as auspicious symbols for the Mandate of Heaven.[58] Indeed, architectural reliefs of trees had a similar role to those of the pillar of heaven

57 *Shanhai jing yizhu* (Shanghai, 2014); Dongfang, *Shenyi jing*, in *Bowu zhi* (*wai qi zhong*).
58 For details, see Tseng, *Picturing Heaven in Early China*, 101–105.

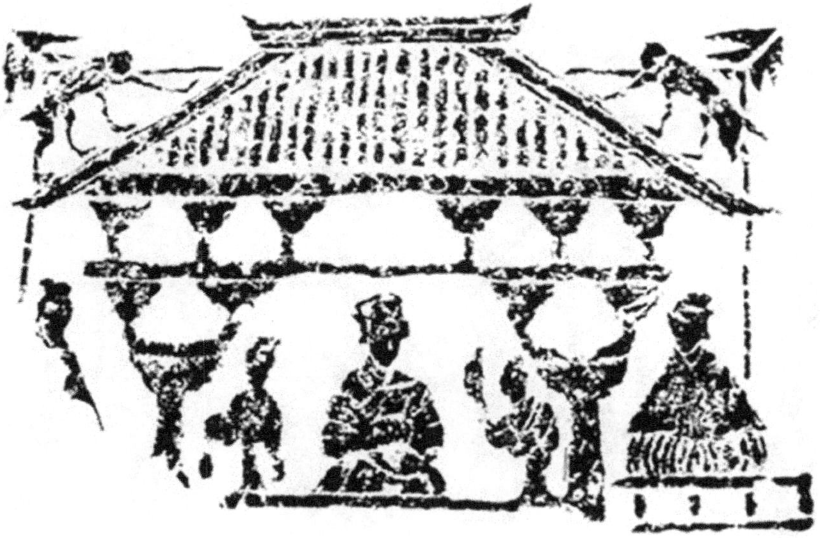

Figure 2.22 Triangular bracket sets, similar to the "inverted mountain" shape, in a rubbing from a Han stone relief from Xuzhou, Jiangsu Province (ZHZYT-J, 53, fig. 2).

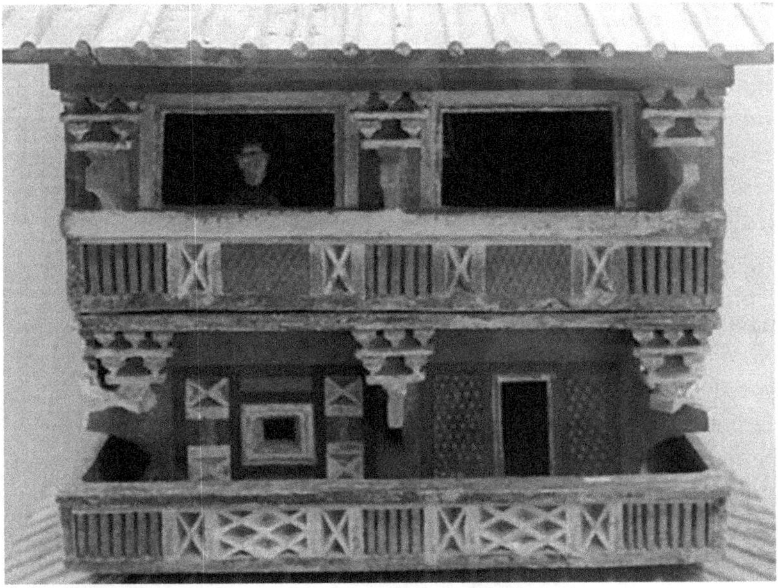

Figure 2.23 Triangular "mountain"-shaped bracket sets in a pottery pavilion from the middle Eastern Han dynasty, unearthed at Mazuo village, Jiaozuo, Henan Province (exhibited in the Ningbo Museum, author's photo, 2019).

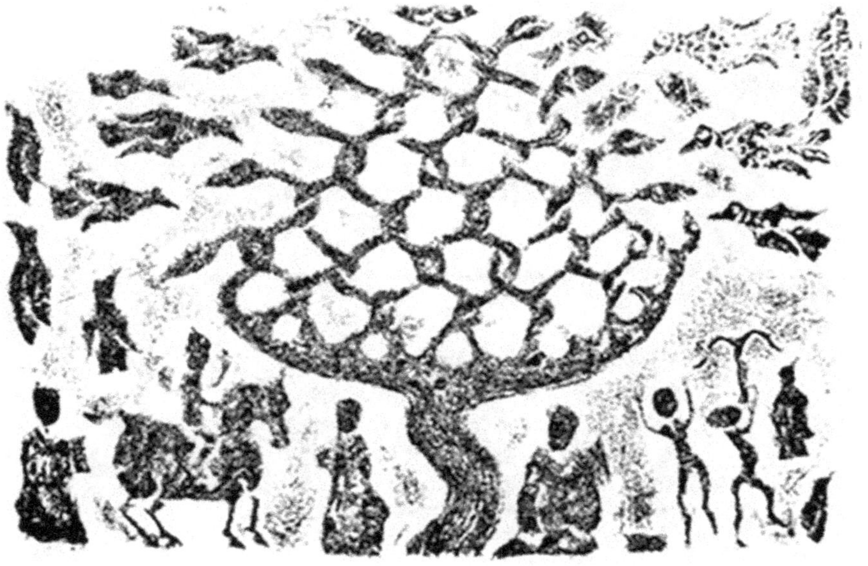

Figure 2.24 Mythical tree in a rubbing from a Han stone relief from Weishan County, Shandong Province (ZHZYT-J, 86, fig. 2).

or Kunlun Mountain, as they all contained divine forces that would elevate the viewer. *Huainan zi* declares that "there is a celestial tree called Jianmu at the legendary place Duguang. From this tree, all the gods would ascend to heaven and descend to the earth."[59] In addition to its verticality, the architectural resemblance of the tree also extended to the bracket set and roof, in the form of blossoming branches and leafy canopy, which could accordingly be interpreted as a means of communicating with heaven. A vivid example of this parallel is recorded in *Shiyi ji*:

> In 549 BCE, the Zhou emperor Lingwang [571–545 BCE] started to build a pavilion called "Kunzhao", also named "Xuanzhao". In the process of assembling precious timbers and marvellous craftsmen, the emperor obtained a tree from the northern area of the E'gu [a valley]. The length of the tree was one thousand *xun* [about 1,848 metres]. With twisted roots and gnarled branches, this single tree alone was sufficient to build the whole pavilion. Therefore the large trunk was used for pillars and beams, while the small branches were used for bracket sets and rafters. The tree itself contained the shapes of dragons, snakes and various

59 Liu, *Huainan zi*, 100.

> beasts. Crystal sand was carefully screened for making the cement. The height of the pavilion reached one hundred *zhang* [about 330 metres]. The emperor would ascend the pavilion to watch the colourful clouds.[60]

The text also mentions a shaman hired by the Zhou court named Chang Hong who could summon immortals. One day the emperor ascended the pavilion and encountered two celestial beings.[61]

Although no built examples of such elevated pavilions survive, numerous stone reliefs and pottery models from the Han dynasty clearly exhibit the social penchant for them (Figures 2.25 and 2.26). Such structures were popular from as early as the Warring States period, as they enabled

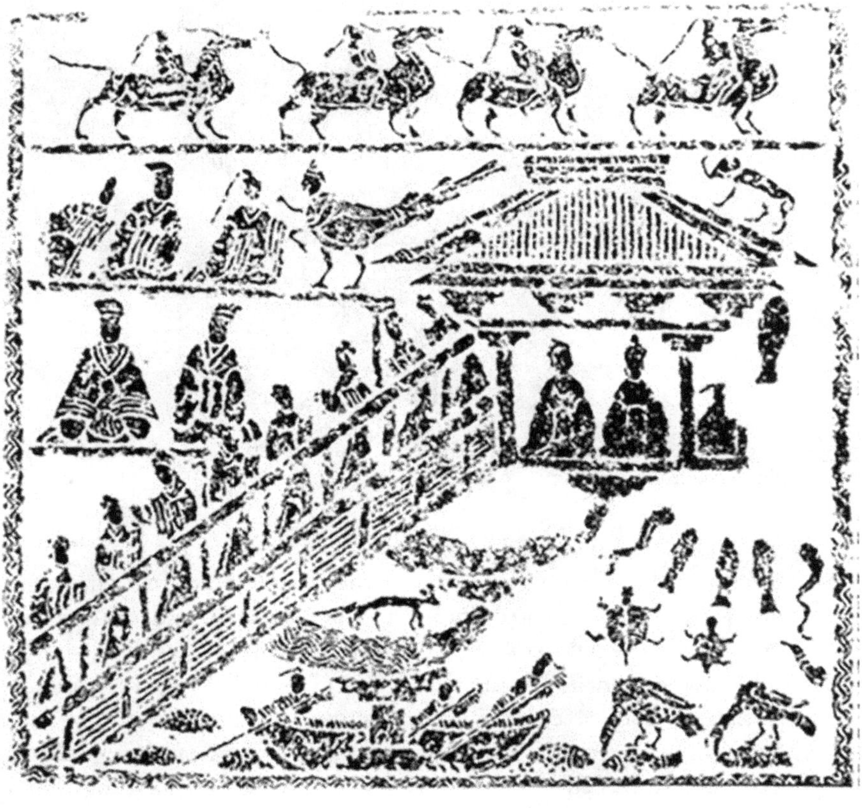

Figure 2.25 Elevated pavilion in a rubbing from a Han stone relief from Weishan County, Shandong Province (ZHZYT-J, 92, fig. 1).

60 Wang, *Shiyi ji*, 73.
61 Ibid., 73–74.

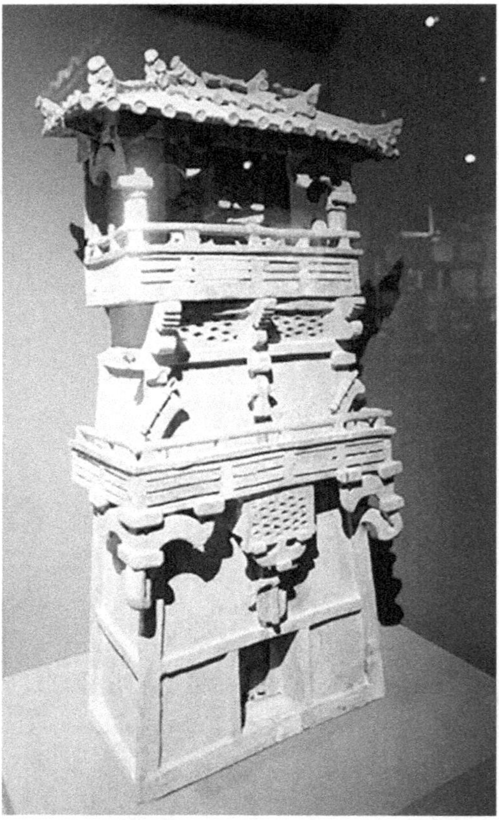

Figure 2.26 Pottery model from the Eastern Han dynasty, unearthed in Chengdu (Chengdu Museum, author's photo, 2016).

the upper classes to showcase their power and wealth.[62] In the Han dynasty, high structures also became symbolic of the desire to attain immortality. They are portrayed as shelters supported by columns and bracket sets, where the deceased would embrace a blessed afterlife. Figure 2.27 shows a bridge-like pavilion elevated by multiple bracket sets that mimic the branching arms of a tree. Such a complicated structure may have had a basis in actual buildings. As recorded in *Bowu zhi* 博物志 (*Records of Diverse Matters*), compiled in the third century, "there is a huge pavilion in Jiangling [Hubei Province]. It has only one column and all the beams are acting as bracket arms to support the whole structure."[63]

62 Chen, *Zhongguo gudai mujiegou jianzhu jishu*, 22.
63 *Bowu zhi*, in *Bowu zhi (wai qi zhong)*, 28.

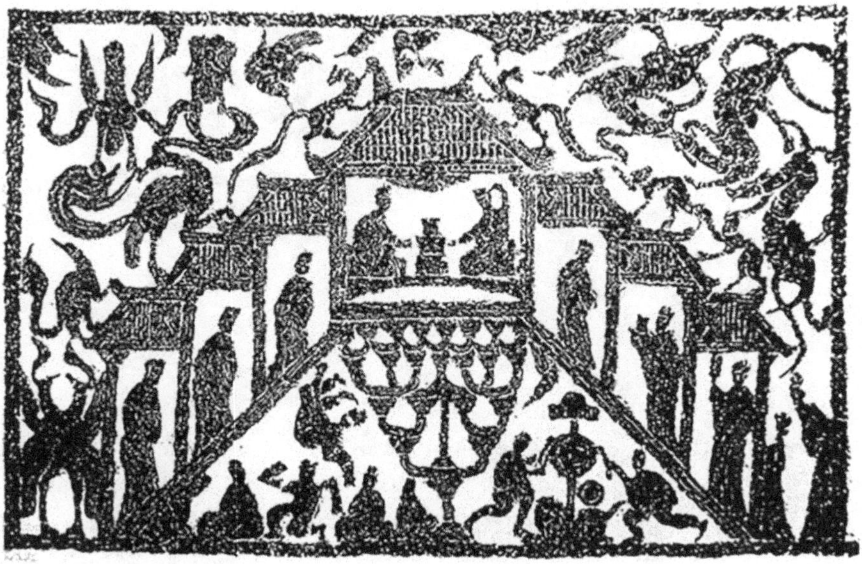

Figure 2.27 Bridge-like pavilion in a Han stone relief from Xuzhou, Jiangsu Province (ZHZYT-J, 144, fig. 2).

Floral and vegetal motifs were characteristic of the architecture of early civilizations. In the Han dynasty, such motifs indicated an auspicious political environment bestowed by heaven and manifest in fertile lands and abundant harvests. The *Da Dai Liji* 大戴礼记 (*Records of Ritual Matters by Dai the Elder*), compiled in the Western Han dynasty, describes the raw material for royal palace buildings in the Zhou dynasty as follows:

> The environment of the Zhou period is full of benevolence, harmony and peace. *Hao* 蒿 [wormwood] grows large and exuberant. It was used for the columns of the palace. Therefore the palace was called Hao Gong 蒿宫 [the Palace of Hao].[64]

Wormwood appears to have had a special resonance in palace architecture. The Chinese character of *hao* in early oracle bone script (late second millennium BCE, see Figure 2.28) suggests that it was grown on both the top and the bottom of tall buildings. The character is similar to that of *gao* 高, which means tall, high, and lofty, by figuratively referring to a building on a high platform. By the time of the Zhou dynasty, however, the character of *hao* had changed

64 Dai De, ed., *Da Dai Liji jinzhu jinyi* (Tianjin, 1975), 293.

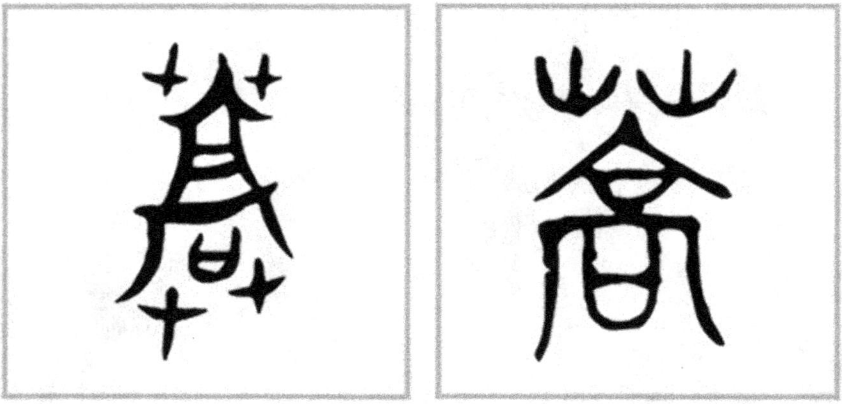

Figure 2.28 The oracle bone (left) and bronzeware (right) characters of *hao* 蒿, from *Han Dian*, zdic.net/z/22/zy/84BF.htm (accessed January 21, 2018).

significantly. As can be seen in bronzeware script of that period (Figure 2.28), the branching component appears only atop the character and now resembles two bracket sets or two mountains, as in the Chinese character of "山."

This element also appears on representations of religious buildings on bronze vessels from the sixth to the fifth centuries BCE, as discussed in the section "Bronzes and religious buildings" in Chapter 1. In the temple depicted on a bronze vase from Changzhi (Shanxi Province), three bracket-like forms similar to the branching components of the *hao* bronze character protrude from its roof ridge (see Figure 1.11). Comparable elements, which Charles D. Weber calls "strange, three-pronged finials," adorn the roof ridge of a religious building on a bronze basin from Hui County, Henan Province (see Figures 1.12).[65] The form of these buildings—a two-story structure surmounted by branching finials—seems to reflect the bronzeware script of *hao* and presumably the legendary Palace of Hao. The form also appears in other building types, and many Han *que* incorporated such three-pronged finials on their roof ridge (see Figures 2.13, 2.29 and 2.30).

---

65 See Charles D. Weber, "Chinese Pictorial Bronze Vessels of the Late Chou Period, Part II," *Artibus Asiae*, 28.4 (1966), 275–277. The iconography of temples includes the depiction of wine vessels located centrally on a table or the floor, sometimes with ladles, and officiants performing rites in different postures. It should be noted that religious buildings and palaces in early China shared the same architecture. As Mark Edward Lewis confirms, elite households and temples were spatially organized according to the same principles: Lewis, *The Construction of Space in Early China* (Albany, NY, 2006), 116–117.

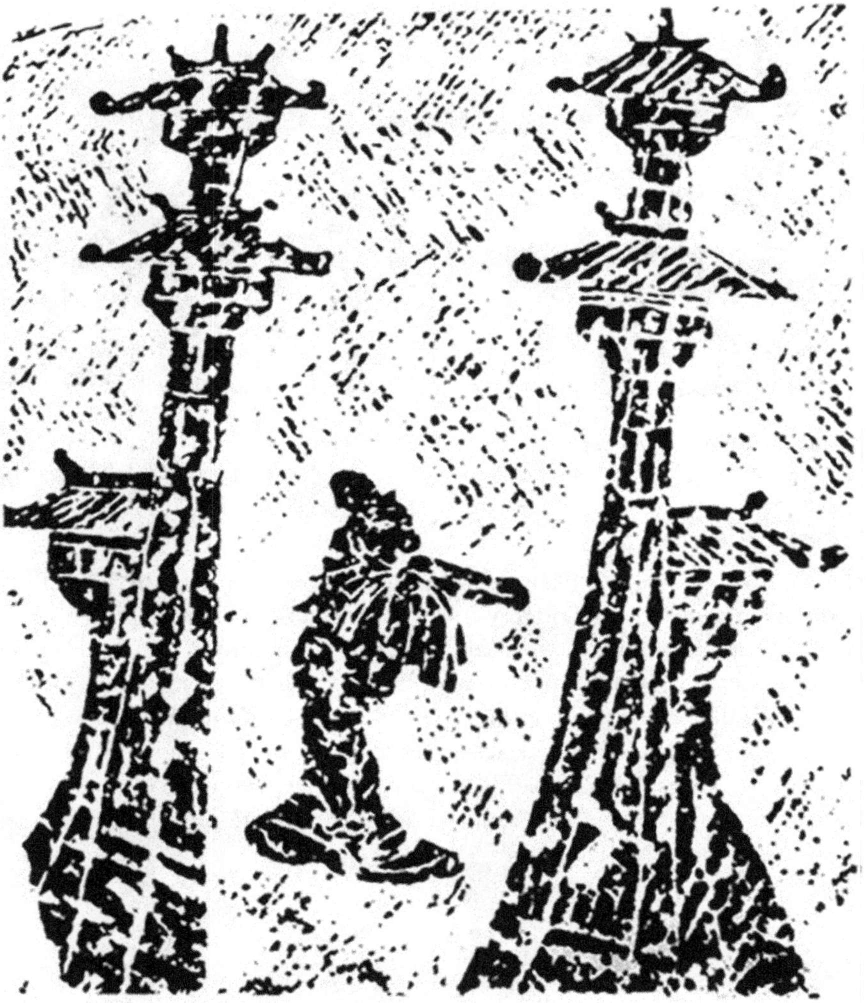

Figure 2.29 Rubbing of a pair of *que*, each with a three-pronged finial on the top, in a Han stone relief from a sarcophagus unearthed in Xinjin County, Sichuan Province (ZHZYT-J, 206, fig. 2).

How are we to explain the similarities between the elements of the *hao* character, the bracket set, and the appearance of that form on roofs? One possible account is that the bracket originated as a symbolic element referring to *hao*, which then transformed over time into a structural element and moved accordingly from the top of the roof ridge to the bottom of

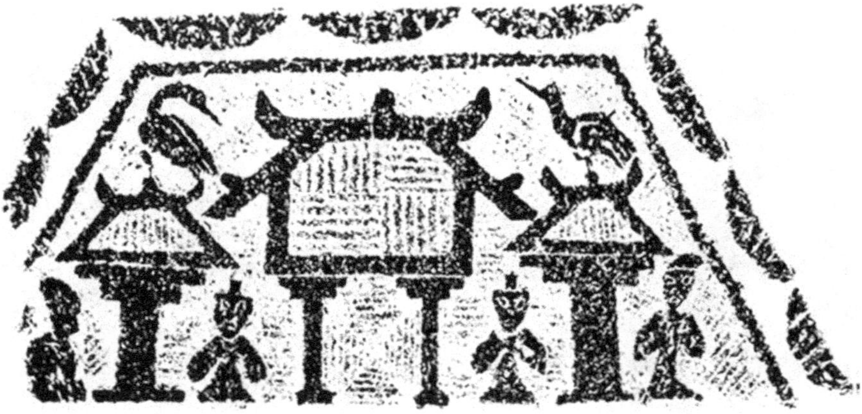

Figure 2.30 Rubbing of a pair of *que* each with a three-pronged finial, from a Han stone relief unearthed in Nanyang County, Henan Province (ZHZYT-J, 223, fig. 1).

the roof beam. A more likely explanation, however, is that the branching component above the roof ridge was only ever ornamental, a re-representation of the actual structure underneath, namely the columns and bracket set holding the roof beams. In a number of Han reliefs, for example, we see great halls illustrated without three-pronged finials. A similar form appears instead as column and bracket sets underneath and supporting the roof structure (Figures 2.31–2.34). These bronze vessels and carved reliefs seem to capture both the symbolic and the structural function of the bracket set in relation to the character *hao*.

Figure 2.31 Han brick relief from Xuchang County, Henan Province (Henan Museum, author's photo, 2021).

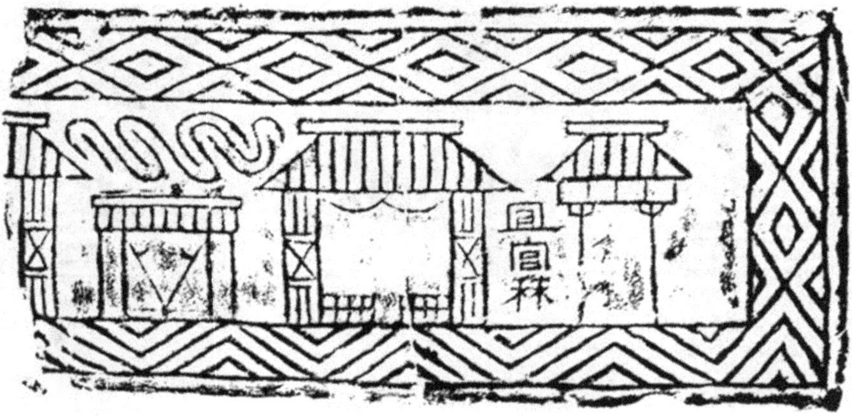

Figure 2.32 Rubbing of a Han stone relief from Xuzhou, Jiangsu Province (ZHZYT-J, 142, fig. 1).

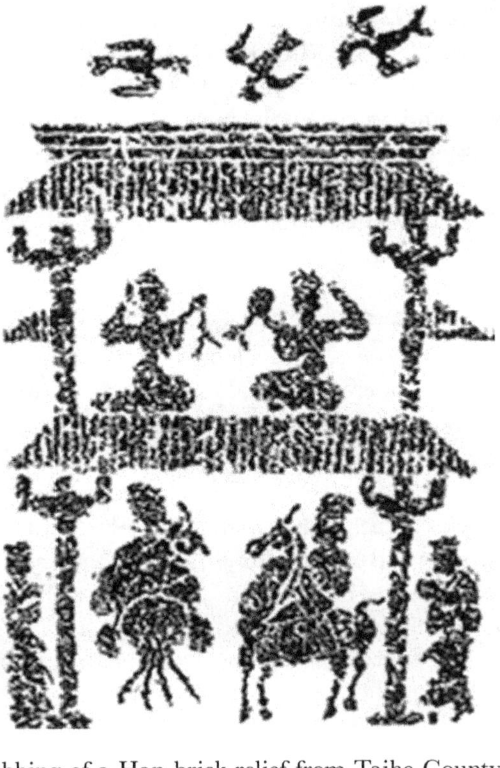

Figure 2.33 Rubbing of a Han brick relief from Taihe County, Anhui Province (ZHZYT-J,11, fig. 3).

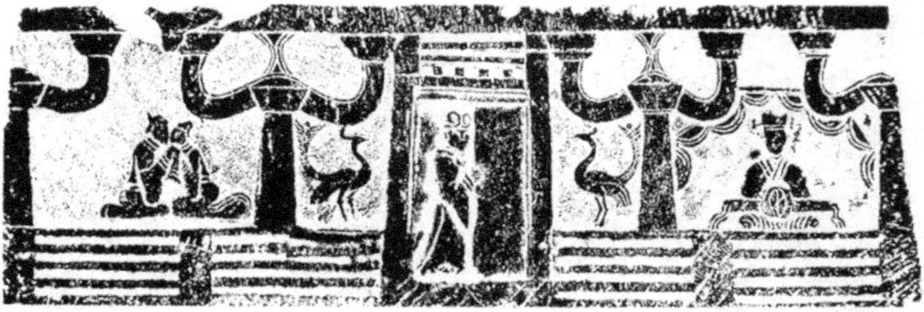

Figure 2.34 Rubbing of a Han stone relief from a sarcophagus unearthed in Yingjing County, Sichuan Province (ZHZYT-J, 42, fig. 1).

There remains the question: why wormwood? As a herb, *hao* is in no way appropriate for building material. The answer is more likely to be found in literary sources than in archaeological ones. In his research on the Palace of Hao, Rao Zongyi points out that the term Hao Gong was first used in *Yanzi chunqiu* 晏子春秋 (*Annals of Master Yan*, c. 500 BCE) in praise of the frugal life of the Zhou emperor. His "Wormwood Palace" was like a thatched cottage made from the leaves of *hao*.[66] In the Han period, however, the symbolism became too lowly, and to meet the imperial demand for grandness and eternity, the humble origin of *hao* in the Zhou palace had to be elevated. To validate and amend the early account quoted in *Da Dai Liji*, the later literature rendered the *hao* used for building the Zhou palace as a celestial plant with miraculous powers. As recorded in *Shiyi ji*,

> There was celestial fleabane growing at Tiaoyang Mountain. Its form was similar to *hao*, yet its length reached ten *zhang* [about 33 metres]. The people offered celestial fleabane as a tribute to the court in the early Zhou dynasty. They were used for the palace columns. Therefore the Zhou palace was called "Hao Gong."[67]

Han and Jin authors clearly felt a political and spiritual need to explain the presence of wormwood as a building material for royal palaces. Such an attempt most likely mirrored a process that had occurred in architecture. The three-pronged form became a marker of important buildings, a transformation that had its origin in the legend of the Palace of Hao.

---

66 Rao Zongyi, "Hao Gong kao," in *Gu'an wenlu* (Shenyang, 2000), 61.
67 Wang, *Shiyi ji*, 66.

As I have argued, columns and bracket sets in the Han period were subject to diverse cosmological and mythical interpretations. They are represented, variously, as pillars of heaven, gates of heaven, the constellations, Kunlun Mountain, and celestial plants.[68] Such diverse architectural interpretations invoke a particular theory of representation. Early Chinese scholars such as Han Fei 韩非 (280?–233 BCE) and Zhang Heng 张衡 (78–139) held that the depiction of invisible things calls for imagination rather than imitation. As Tseng has argued, Han artisans adopted this approach in their attempts to depict heaven.[69] Architecture, too, was employed in this effort. The column and bracket set served as an effective representation of celestial and spiritual qualities.

Dougong in Succeeding Dynasties

The development of wooden column and bracket sets reached its apogee in the Tang–Song period (618–1279), particularly with the evolution of *dougong* into multilayered clusters, or *chonggong*. In his study of *dougong*, Han Baode, guided by a modernist and rationalist approach to structure, questioned the redundancy inherent in the multiple *dougong* system.[70] Jiren Feng's research on Song architecture partly answers Han's criticism.[71] To Feng, columns with multilayered *dougong* brackets functioned as an architectural metaphor: like trees, they represented a natural force of growth applicable both to the form of the roof and to the fortunes of the household. The symbol of prosperity was an appealing and perpetual theme in Chinese culture. Not surprisingly, Feng also found evidence for the analogy between the bracket set and flora during the Han period.[72] As I have argued, however, the range of meanings inherent in *dougong* was originally much broader.

In succeeding dynasties, the diverse celestial and mythical connotations of Han architecture narrowed to a predominant, terrestrial one, a process most likely driven by an increasingly rational and mathematical approach to carpentry. As Chen Mingda has shown, it was during the Tang–Song dynasties that the technology of timber reached its highest level of standardization and modularization.[73] The key term in *Yingzao fashi* (chapters four and five)

68 For an analogous reading of *dougong* in relation to the Five Element theory (*wuxing*), see Liu Jie, *Jiangnan mugou* (Shanghai, 2009), 136–144.
69 Tseng, *Picturing Heaven in Early China*, 1.
70 Han, *Ming-Qing jianzhu er'lun/Dougong de qiyuan yu fazhan*, 87–132.
71 Feng, *Chinese Architecture and Metaphor*, 138–180.
72 Ibid., 144–145, 161, 168–179.
73 Chen, *Zhongguo gudai mujiegou jianzhu jishu*, 59.

is the structural unit or *cai*, which referred to the size of the timber cross section and from which all dimensional measurements followed. In a sense, the scale of a building was determined by the selection of the grade of *cai*.[74] It is not difficult to see how such a practical and instrumental approach to architecture would have replaced a transcendent and other-worldly one. This transformation may also explain the much-reduced audience for such architectural metaphors. The written sources that Feng presents were probably exchanged only among some interested literati and a few knowledgeable craftsmen.

Legislation limiting the use of *dougong* as a means of articulating social hierarchy may also have played a role in restricting its range of meaning. As stated in the Introduction, sumptuary codes from the Tang to the Ming dynasties (c. 618–1644) indicated that *chonggong* (*dougong* in multiple forms) were excluded from the commoner's houses. There was also a differentiation between royal family members and court officials in adopting *chonggong* in their houses. Such social codification of the *dougong* system would inevitably lead to a standardized or somewhat simplified representational function.

The later history of *dougong* is too large a subject to treat here, beyond more than a brief overview. During the twelfth century, the structural use of *chonggong* in major buildings declined, even while the number of layers and complexity of the form increased.[75] The periods following the Song dynasty saw a continued reduction in the contribution of *chonggong* to structure so that by the time of the Qing dynasty (1636/1644–1912), *dougong* had virtually become an element of pure decoration.[76] That is not to say that the development of bracket sets lacked innovation. We can see subtle progress in their structural function and decorative features, even as they became smaller, more rigid and formulaic.[77] As Guo Huayu has shown, this process entailed a number of social and architectural factors concerning structural load, the integrity of multiple layers, anti-seismic attributes, ornament, and social standing.[78] Further studies should verify whether the "vegetal" metaphor prevalent during the Song dynasty continued into later periods. They may help to explain, from a cultural perspective, the longevity of *dougong* in architecture throughout the imperial period.

---

74 Li Jie, *Yingzao fashi* (Beijing, 2011), 29–43; Qinghua Guo, "Yingzao Fashi: Twelfth-Century Chinese Building Manual," *Architectural History* 41 (1998), 6–7.

75 Zhong Xiaoqing, "Dougong, puzuo, yu puzuo ceng," 26.

76 Liang and Liu, "Dougong jianshuo," 295, 312.

77 For a comparative study of *dougong* between the Song and Qing dynasties, with precise physical measurements of their components, see Yu Zhuoyun, "Dougong de yunyong shi woguo gudai jianzhu jishu de zhongyao gongxian," in: *Zhongguo gongdian jianzhu lunwen ji* (Beijing, 2002), 165–193.

78 Guo Huayu, *Zhongguo gudian jianzhu xingzhi yuanliu* (Wuhan, 2015), 235–238.

Dougong in Modern Times

In the early twentieth century, there was a return of interest in the imperial construction manuals among Chinese scholars and architects. As Li Shiqiao has demonstrated, there were several attempts to reprint, edit, and annotate *Yingzao fashi* in particular, each an attempt to define Chinese architecture as a critical response to Western influence.[79] Among these efforts, the drawing and annotation of *dougong* was a major focus.[80] Through the 1920s, many Chinese architects returned from overseas and began to develop a more scientific and systematic approach to preserving historic buildings. The surveys conducted by the Society for the Study of Chinese Architecture had an especially long-lasting influence on historic preservation in China.[81]

There persists a cautious struggle among Chinese scholars and architects to claim a cultural identity in modern architectural practice. This struggle, which is becoming more apparent as China surges as a driver of the global economy and of geopolitics, is manifested in two architectural trends. One is historic preservation and its related heritage-led urban regeneration. Significant historic buildings have been enlisted in government preservation catalogues and properly preserved. There are also numerous counterfeit historic structures, built using traditional materials and construction methods to satisfy heritage conservation purposes, if only superficially. The other approach is a creative revival of Chinese traditional elements in contemporary architecture. For example, the China Pavilion in Shanghai and the Guotai Arts Centre in Chongqing are cases where the traditional *dougong* system has undergone different modern architectural interpretations. Traditional columns and *dougong* also appear in some major public buildings. Nanjing South Railway Station (Jiangsu Province) and Jixi North Station (Anhui Province), for example, both use steel to reinterpret the columns and *dougong* system.

Practice and research on architectural heritage in China today continue apace. Yet architecture in modern society, as Yi-Fu Tuan argues, is unable to heighten religious significance, or to exemplify a totalizing worldview.[82] By reconstructing the cosmological and mythical belief system of the Han dynasty as expressed by the column and bracket set, this chapter argues that Chinese architecture was once closely bonded to the heavens.

---

79 Li Shiqiao, "Reconstituting Chinese Building Tradition: The *Yingzao fashi* in the Early Twentieth Century," *Journal of the Society of Architectural Historians*, 62.4 (2003), 470–489.

80 See, in particular, Liang Sicheng's meticulous documentation of the *dougong* system as described by Li Jie in *Yingzao fashi*: Liang Sicheng, ed., *Qing Gongbu gongcheng zuofa zeli tujie* (Beijing, 2006).

81 For more details, see Jing Xie and Tim Heath, *Heritage-Led Urban Regeneration in China* (New York and London, 2017), 16–21.

82 Yi-Fu Tuan, *Space and Place: The Perspective of Experience* (Minneapolis, MN, 2008), 112–113.

Chapter 3

THE ORIGIN AND DEVELOPMENT OF *ZAOJING*

Widely evident in the great halls from imperial China, and exhibiting superb craftsmanship, *zaojing* are taken for granted as symbols of prestige (see Figures 2–4). Some researchers affirm that *zaojing* were a product of Confucianism, as it helped to emphasize the unity of heaven and man on the one hand, and a hierarchical society on the other.[1] Situated in a central position of a ceiling, *zaojing* may be a square, an octagon, or a circle, among a number of shapes. Equivalent to domes of heaven in the Western context,[2] *zaojing* were believed to have a magic power protecting the architecture and inhabitants it enshrined. In particular, a *zaojing* was built within a structure to prevent the building from fire, an urban disaster that frequently took place in the past. Focusing on the archeological and literary sources from early China, this chapter inquiries about the origin of *zaojing* and attempts to articulate how *zaojing* evolved as an architectural means to assuage human fears, as well as to express human desires and longing.

Zaojing and Water Well

Both the physical form and the literary term *jing* 井 suggest that *zaojing* had an inherent connection with a water well. To further illustrate this linkage, a Neolithic water well in the Hemudu cultural relic site (modern Yuyao, Zhejiang Province) is selected as a case study (Figure 3.1). The plan of this well consists of an irregular circle on the periphery and a square in the center

---

1 For example, see Han Yu and Guo Hongwu, "Confucianism in Caisson," *Furniture Interior Design*, no. 10 (2010): 40–41; Zhang Shuxian, "The transformation and cultural meanings of zaojing in ancient Chinese architecture," *World of Antiquity*, 6 (2003): 35–41.

2 This relation has been discussed by Alexander Coburn Soper, "The 'Dome of Heaven' in Asia," *The Art Bulletin*, 29, no. 4 (1947): 225–248, and also by Steinhardt, *Chinese Architecture in an Age of Turmoil* (Honolulu, 2014), 270–283.

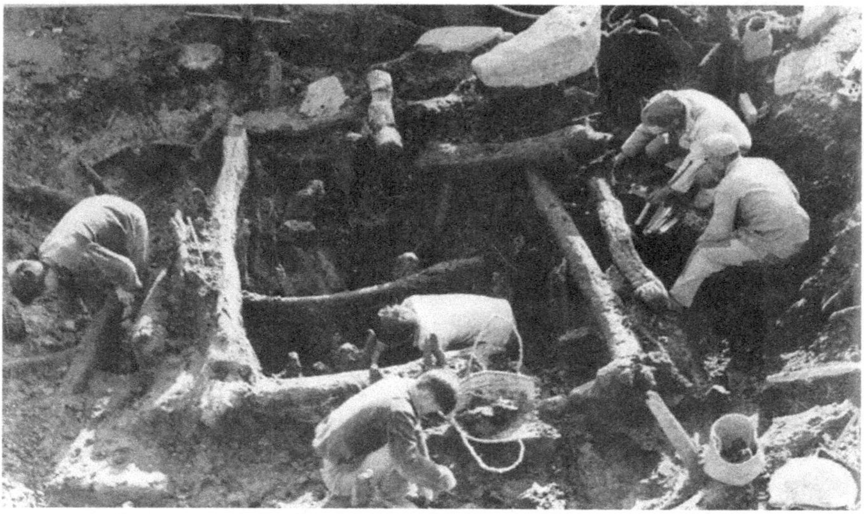

Figure 3.1 The archaeological excavation of the Neolithic water well in the Hemudu archaeological site in 1973 (photo courtesy of the Museum of Yuyao Hemudu Relic).

(Figure 3.2). Viewing the section, the circle is actually the surface of a basin that was full of water during the flooding season.[3]

With a side length of two meters, the square is a shaft that sinks to the bottom of the basin, thereby forming a water well. During periods of drought, the well continued as a water source. Circular and semicircular wooden piles, whose diameters are about six centimeters, were densely erected against the four internal sides of the well. They were then reinforced by a square frame constructed by four horizontally laid round logs, each with a diameter of about 17 centimeters (see Figure 3.2). These four wooden logs were assembled with tenon and mortise joints.[4] The wooden structure of the well, particularly its square frame on the upper edge, reflects the early pictograph character of *jing* (Figure 3.3).

This form of the wooden construction of a well is also identifiable in the Shang dynasty. Two water wells from that period have been unearthed in Taixi village (Shijiazhuang, Hebei Province), which clearly contain a

3 Zhejiang Culture Relics Management Committee and Zhejiang Provincial Museum, "Hemudu yizhi diyiqi fajue baogao," *Kaogu Xuebao*, 1 (1978): 49–51.

4 See ibid. and Yang Hongxun, "Hemudu yizhi mugou shuijing jianding," in: *Jianzhu kaoguxue lunwenji* (Beijing, 1987), 52–57.

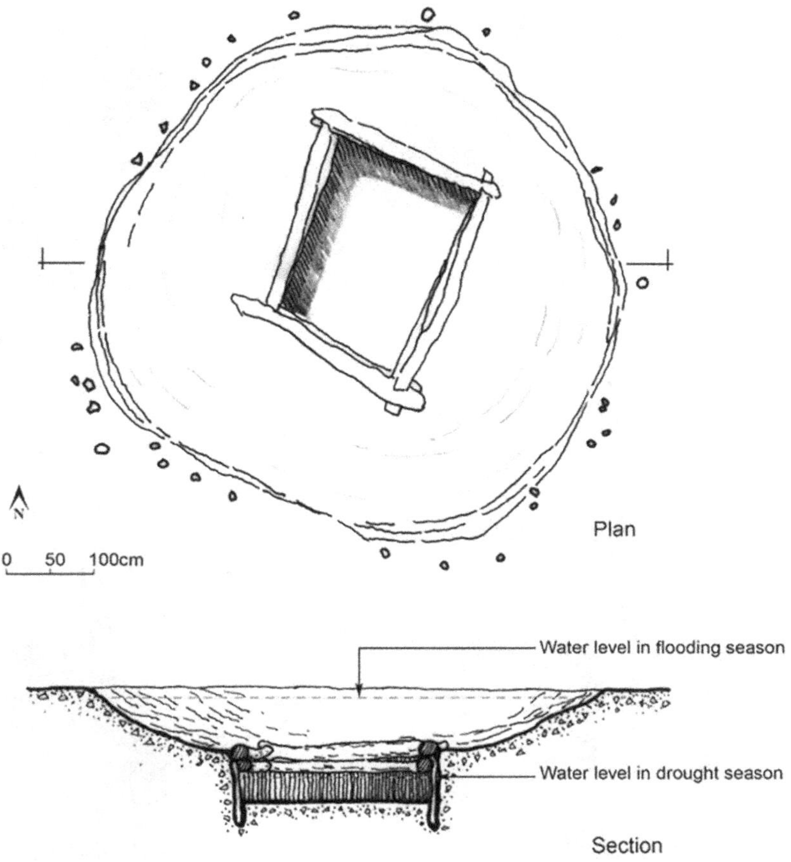

Figure 3.2 Plan and section of the water well at the Hemudu site (author's drawing, 2019, based on the site survey and *Jianzhu kaoguxue lunwenji* (Beijing, 1987), 54, fig. 2).

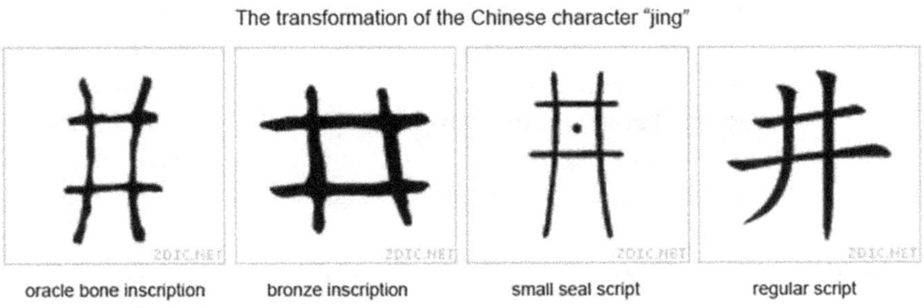

Figure 3.3 The transformation of the character *jing*, in *Han Dian*, http://www.zdic.net/z/15/zy/4E95.htm (access April 21, 2018).

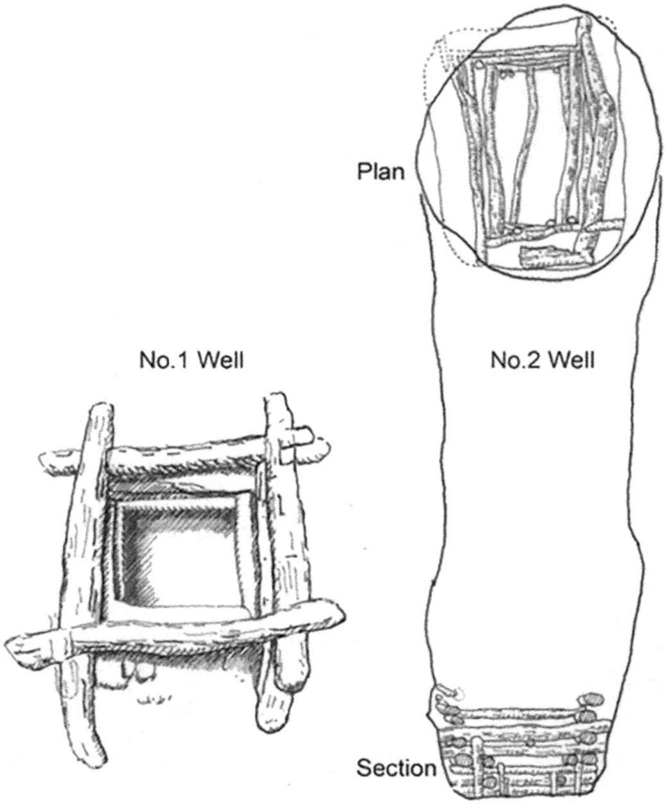

Figure 3.4 The two Shang water wells in Taixi village (author's drawing, 2019, based on *Gaocheng Taixi Shang dai yizhi*, 68–70, figs. 51 and 53).

wooden structure that resembles the character of *jing* (Figure 3.4).[5] The early construction of dry wells also followed the same principle. In the ancient mining site unearthed in Tonglü Mountain (Hubei Province), for example, there are a number of mining wells whose history can be traced back to the Spring and Autumn Period. The four wooden piles were joined together in the shape of '井', which was a basic structural unit for the construction of the vertical mining wells and horizontal tunnels (Figure 3.5).[6]

5 Hebei Provincial Museum, Taixi archeology brigade, Theoretic team of Taixi brigade in Gaocheng County, *Gaocheng Taixi Shang dai yizhi* (Beijing, 1977), 66–71.

6 Yin Weizhang, "Excavation report of the Eastern Zhou copper mining relic in Tonglü Mountain Hubei," *Kaogu*, 1 (1981): 20.

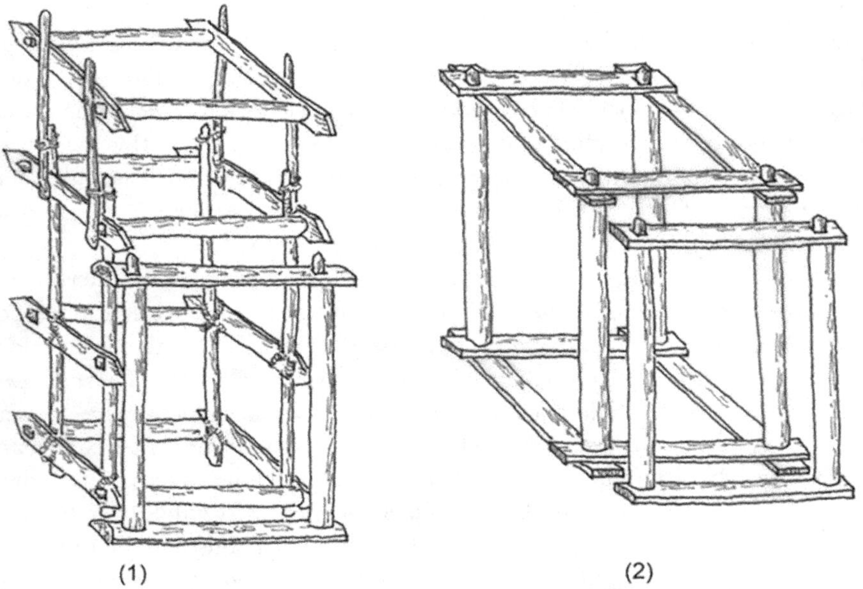

Figure 3.5 The wooden structure for both vertical mining well (1) and horizontal tunnels (2) in Tonglü Mountain, Hubei Province (author's drawing, 2019, based on *Kaogu*, 1 (1981), 20, fig. 1).

The characteristic wooden construction of a well is conspicuously retained in both the oracle bone inscription and bronze inscription of *jing* 井 (see Figure 3.3). This, in conjunction with the archaeological discovery of the wells discussed above, leads Yang Hongxun to assert that such a particular wooden structure, called "jing gan" 井幹 in the ancient literature, prevailed throughout the Shang and Zhou dynasties.[7] Yang further points out that the early meaning of a water well also implies its physical construction. The term "*jing* means pellucid, that is, it is a purifier for spring water,"[8] and by quoting the meaning of *jing* in the Han lexicon *Shiming* 释名, Yang claims that the wooden frame inside a primitive well acted as a retaining wall, which also prevented the mud from the pit mixing with water, thereby maintaining its clear quality.[9]

Much evidence from the Han dynasty further suggests an inherent link between the textural and structural forms of *jing*. By this time, *jing* had a collection

7 Yang, "Hemudu yizhi mugou shuijing jianding," 55.
8 Liu Xi, *Shiming* (Beijing, 2016), 83.
9 Yang, "Hemudu yizhi mugou shuijing jianding," 55–56.

of meanings. In *Shuowen jiezi* 说文解字, *jing* first means a neighborhood unit, that is, eight households sharing a water well.[10] As the small seal script of *jing* in Figure 3.3 shows, two sets of parallel lines crossing each other divides a square into nine blocks. The section in the central block represents the water source and the surrounding blocks refer to eight households. In this sense, *jing* suggests a strict administrative order which most likely preconditioned the later development of one particular type of *zaojing* that assumed a chessboard pattern—a reproduction of the character of *jing* (Figure 3.6).

As in early times, in the Han period, *jing* also figuratively referred to the wooden structure of a water well, yet by this time the structure had appeared above the ground in the form of a balustrade. As stated in the annotation of *jing* in *Shuowen jiezi*, the geometrical strokes of the Chinese character *jing* refer to the wooden balustrade of a water well, whose shape assumes either a quadrangle or an octagon.[11] The physical configuration of a well can be verified by a number of stone reliefs from the Han dynasty. One relief in a Han tomb unearthed in Beizhai village, Shandong Province from the late second century, for example, shows an illustration of a house (see Figure 2.11). The front court contains a well on one side, indicated by the presence of a balustrade proclaiming the character of *jing* but with a windlass above, too.

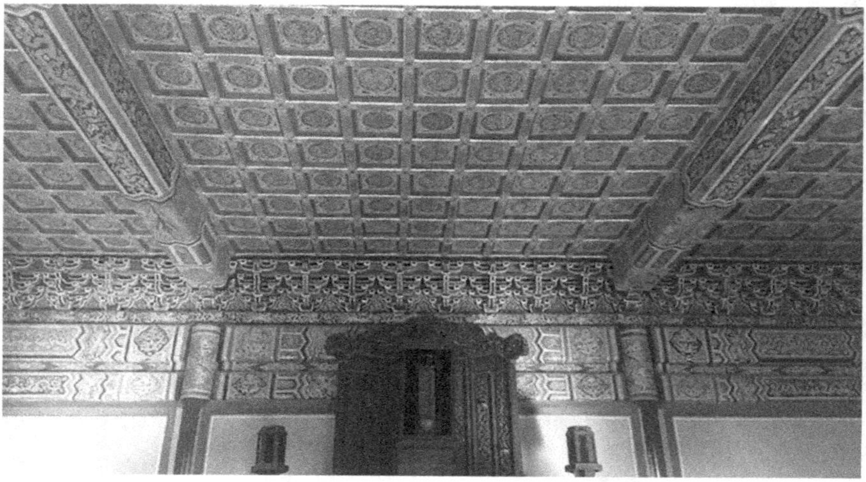

Figure 3.6 *Zaojing* in Imperial Hall of Heaven (皇乾殿, Huangqian dian), in Temple of Heaven, Beijing, built between 1406 and 1420, and renovated between 1750 and 1790 (author's photo, 2012).

10 *Shuowen jiezi zhu* (Shanghai, 2019), 216.
11 Ibid.

Similarly, another Han relief unearthed in Zengjiabao, Chengdu also depicts a well with its raised frame constructed in the shape of *jing* (Figure 3.7).

The importance of a well was further underlined by many pottery models of wells appearing as numinous objects in Han tombs offering their service to the afterlife of the deceased. The cap structure of a well forming the character *jing* sometimes was unnecessarily exaggerated (Figure 3.8). For building a well in the Han dynasty, stone masonry was widely available according to archaeological findings. Interestingly, the detail of Han pottery wells, as Guo Qinghua urges, requires particular attention: "the well head was made to imitate a log structure notched together at the four corners, with heads and sills protruding beyond the joints."[12] Indeed the early wooden form

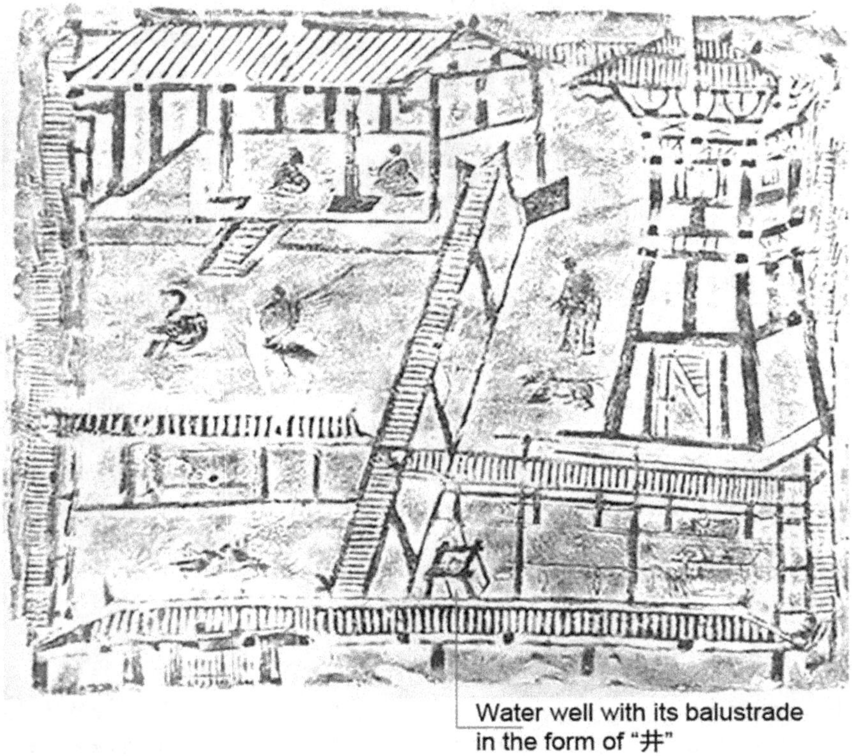

Figure 3.7 The courtyard house from the relief sculpture in Zengjiabao tomb from the Eastern Han period, unearthed in Chengdu, Sichuan Province, exhibited in Chengdu Museum (author's photo, 2016).

12 Qinghua Guo, *The mingqi Pottery Buildings of Han Dynasty China 206 BC–AD 220: Architectural Representation and Represented Architecture* (Brighton, 2010), 116–117.

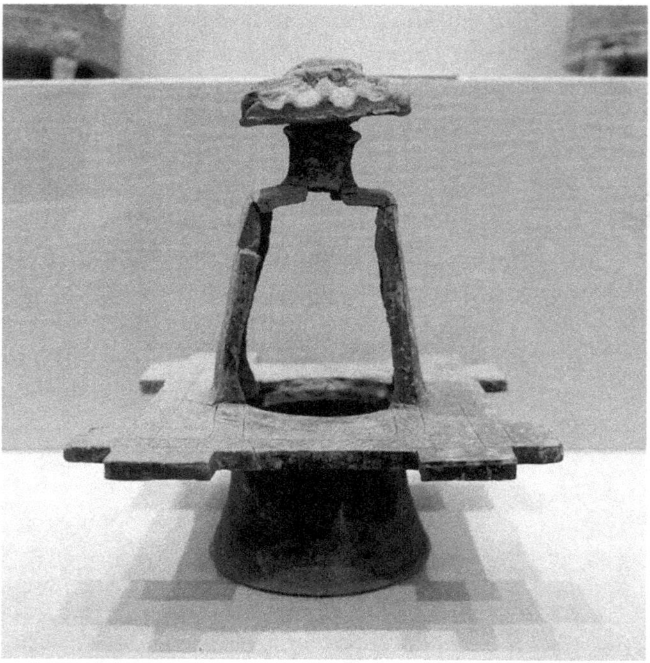

Figure 3.8 A pottery model of a water well from the Han period, unearthed in Xinxiang, Henan Province (Zhengzhou Museum, author's photo, 2021).

of *jing* (i.e., four wooden piles crossing each other to form a square frame) was conspicuously retained as an essential feature that defined the very existence of a well. From the above discussion of the epistemic linkage between the Chinese character of *jing* and the physical form of wells, we can develop an argument to show that the physical structure of a well provides a prototype for the later development of *zaojing* on ceilings.

Zaojing and Skylight

Regarding the origin of *zaojing*, one theory is that it started as an opening on the top of a primitive hut (or cave) providing natural light and smoke exhaust.[13] Primitive people are believed to have lived in huts or caves. In the need

---

13 The term "primitive" used in this chapter carries the same connotation as Joseph Rykwert's discussion on primitive hut, see Rykwert, *On Adam's House in Paradise: The Idea of the Primitive Hut in Architectural History* (Cambridge, MA, 1981).

for interior illumination and ventilation, a circular opening on the top of a dwelling was introduced. The Neolithic houses unearthed in Banpo village, Xi'an, for example, erected with wooden piles and cladded with an earth and straw mixture, took an either round or quadrangular shape; inside, there was a vertical connection between the hearth on the ground and the opening above (Figure 3.9).[14]

The central location and functional importance of such opening in time acquired a particular term *zhongliu* 中霤 that first appeared in *Chunqiu Gongyang zhuan* 春秋公羊传 from the early Han dynasty. In his annotation to *Chunqiu gongyang zhuan*, the Tang scholar Xu Yan 徐彥 stated that *zhongliu* was the center of a room for worshipping purpose and the term was derived from the ancient caves, a type of dwelling that was covered by earth. By quoting from another scholar Yu Wei 庾蔚, Xu further explained that these ancient caves all had a central opening on their roof through which rainwater would flow down. This was the literal meaning of *liu*, that is, rainwater dripping. The central room was thus named as *zhongliu* (central dripping).[15]

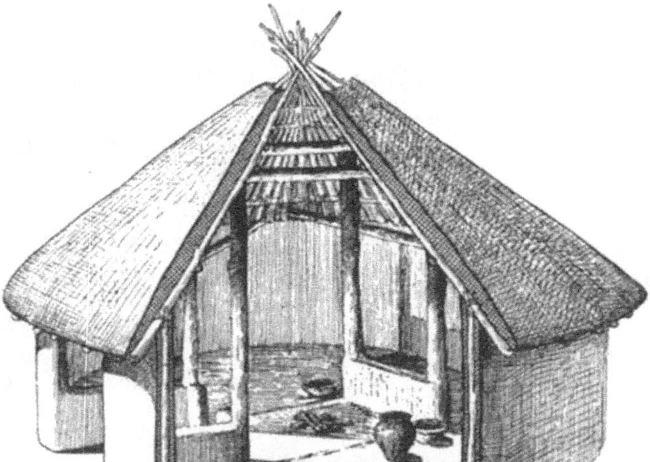

Figure 3.9 The restoration illustration of the no. 22 circular hut in Banpo village, Xi'an, Shaanxi Province (Banpo Museum, Xi'an, author's photo, 2021).

14 The Institute of Archeology, Chinese Academy of Sciences and Shaanxi Xi'an Banpo Museum, *Xi'an Banpo* (Beijing, 1963).

15 He Xiu and Xu Yan, *Chunqiu Gongyang zhuan zhushu* (Shanghai, 2014), 1159.

The term *zhongliu* also appeared in the Han lexicon *Shiming* which confirmed that the character of *liu* 霤 was derived from the name of an ancient dwelling and was interchangeable with the character of *liu* 流, meaning water flowing from the top of a house into the interior.[16] Yet in the Han period, *zhongliu* referred to a central position underneath the ridgepole of a house, that is, right beneath the oculus in a primitive hut.[17] The explanation of the term "liu" was echoed in *Shuowen jiezi*, which not only quoted the exact text from *Shiming* to explain *zhongliu*, but also emphasized that "liu" meant there was flowing water in a house.[18]

The varying definitions of *zhongliu* in the Han lexicons were most likely due to the housing transformation from primitive hut (or cave) to traditional house. In this process, openings were introduced on walls and *zhongliu* perhaps lost its function for ventilation and daylighting. Yet the symbolic meaning of *zhongliu* in the Han period as the center of a house or precisely as the locus dedicated to the household god was reinforced. The Eastern Han scholar Ban Gu 班固 (32–92) recorded that there were five sacrifices in a senior court official's household: worshipping the gate, doors/windows, well, hearth, and *zhongliu*.[19] In fact, as early as the Spring and Autumn Period, worship of *zhongliu* was well documented. For example, *Liji* 礼记 (*Book of Rites*) wrote that "the major god (the god of earth) for a household is called 'zhongliu' and for a state is called 'she' 社."[20] Also, for the worship of *zhongliu*, the hearts of livestock should be a specific offering.[21]

The origin and transformation of *zhongliu* seem to be a fascinating topic that has drawn the attention of the Chinese historian Gu Jiegang who affirms that the fenestration of primitive huts was the origin of *zhongliu*.[22] Drawing inspiration from his visits to Mongolian yurts, historic courtyard houses, and archaeological sites, Gu asserts that within a primitive hut, there was a central receptacle on the ground corresponding to the *zhongliu* above so that the rainwater would not drench the entire floor.[23] This type of vertical connection later on developed into a courtyard setting, which was termed

16 Liu, *Shiming*, 82.
17 Ibid., 78.
18 *Shuowen jiezi zhu*, 573.
19 Ban Gu, *Hanshu* (Xi'an, 2006), 131.
20 *Liji yizhu* (Shanghai, 2016), 389.
21 Ibid., 248.
22 Gu Jiegang, "zhongliu you fuxue lai," in: *Gu Jiegang quanji* (Beijing, 2011), vol. 24, ch. 9, 228.
23 Gu Jiegang, *Shilin zashi* (Beijing, 1963), 140–145.

as *tianjing* 天井 (sky well) that figuratively suggests the rainwater falling down from the surrounding eaves.[24] Such enclosed space itself also resembles a large well, as Ronald Knapp points out that:

> Standing in the center of most *tianjing*, described in Chinese as *jingdi zhi wa* 井底之蛙 [a frog at the bottom of a well], one typically has only a limited outlook and can see merely a patch of the sky directly above.[25]

Indeed, the term *liu*, initially meaning the central opening where water flowed into, subsequently referred to the eaves of a house. This was verified by the Qing scholar Jiao Xun 焦循 in his architectural treatise *Qunjing gongshi tu* 群经宫室图. Through reviewing the writings from early times, Jiao pointed out that *liu* was essentially the eaves of a house.[26] In a quadrangular setting, four eaves are curving down from four pinnacles of a traditional roof, thereby physically facilitating the water flow (Figure 3.10). According to Jiao, having the architectural feature *liu* in a household was really an upper-class practice.[27] The presence of *liu* in a roof structure partially explained the Chinese penchant for adopting the curved overhanging roof (i.e., four corners of a roof curving up toward the sky) in most important buildings.

The shifting location of *liu* is also indicated by the changing venue of ritual within a house. This is evident in the courtyard where formal household rites take place, such as, worshipping ancestors, weddings, and coming-of-age ceremonies. In a written communication with Gu Jiegang, the scholar Meng Mowen agreed with Gu's theory of *zhongliu*, writing that:

> the system of *zhongliu* has developed from small to large, from skylight to sky well, and from sky well to courtyard. Although the form of *zhongliu* dramatically changed, its original function [as a place for worship] remains consistent.[28]

Compared to its discreet origin as an oculus (i.e., *zhongliu*), the courtyard in traditional Chinese architecture is taken for granted as the most important

24 Ibid.
25 Ronald Knapp, *China's Old Dwellings* (Honolulu, 2000), 46–49.
26 Jiao Xun, *Qunjing gongshi tu* (printed in the Qing dynasty).
27 Ibid.
28 Cited in Gu, *Shilin zashi*, 144.

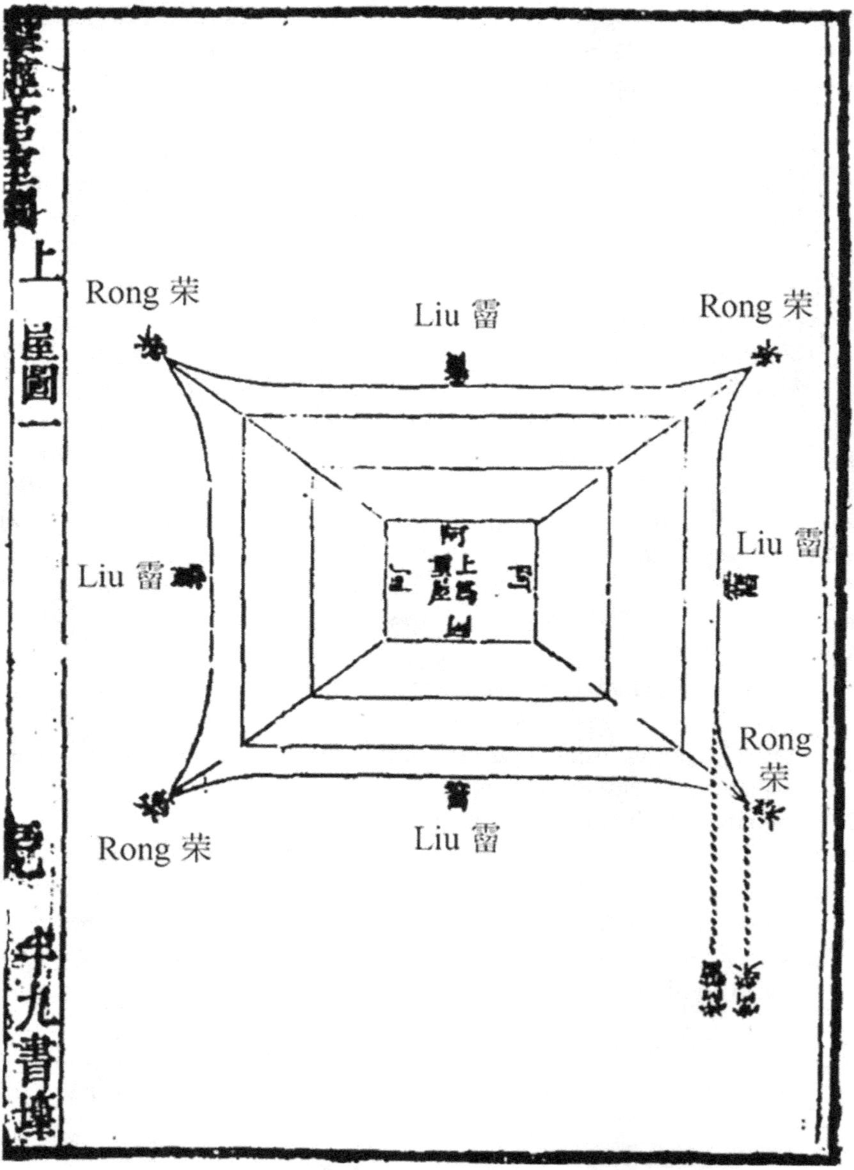

Figure 3.10 *Liu* illustrated by the Qing scholar Jiao Xun (from Jiao Xun, *Qunjing gongshi tu*, housing diagram no. 1).

element of a civilized household.[29] As mentioned in Chapter 2, according to the early Confucian lexicon *Erya*, the courtyard was the place for the ruler to conduct official audiences, with a rigid hierarchy of positioning the court officials being the rule.[30] The influential early twentieth-century theologian, Rudolf Otto, even selected the Chinese courtyard to elaborate his concept of the numinous. He states:

> Chinese architecture, which is essentially an art in the laying out and grouping of buildings, makes a wise and very striking use of this fact [i.e. silence]. It does not achieve the impression of solemnity by lofty vaulted halls or imposing altitudes, but nothing could well be more solemn than the silent amplitude of the enclosed spaces, courtyards, and vestibules [...][31]

This is echoed by Yi-Fu Tuan. In comparing the interior of grand Chinese temples with a light-animated Gothic cathedral, Tuan comments: "In traditional Chinese architecture, the nearest to a sublime interior is the great courtyard, closed to the profane world but open to the sky."[32]

The *zhongliu* of a primitive hut from early China did not evolve into the oculus, such as that of the Pantheon, in association with the splendid concrete dome. Rather, *zhongliu* opened itself up and expanded into a courtyard, becoming a space of inhabitation that directly connected to the sky—the dome of heaven in the Chinese cosmological viewpoint.[33] Without referencing Gu Jiegang, the modern scholar Sun Zongwen also enquires about the meaning of *zhongliu*, confirming the inherent linkage between *zhongliu* in a primitive hut and the sky well (or courtyard) in a traditional house.[34] In the shift of ritual venue within a house, *zaojing* was most likely a product of reminiscence, symbolically reflecting the preexistence of *zhongliu* within a building.

---

29 For detailed study on Chinese courtyards, please see Xing Ruan, *Confucius' Courtyard* (London, 2022).

30 *Erya yizhu* (Shanghai, 2012), 210.

31 Rudolf Otto, *The Idea of the Holy: An Inquiry into the Non-Rational Factor in the Idea of the Divine and Its Relation to the Rational* (Beijing, 1999), 69.

32 Yi-Fu Tuan, *Humanist Geography: An Individual's Search for Meaning* (Staunton, VA, 2012), 98.

33 Jun Hu has discussed extensively that the early Chinese literature often portrayed the shape of the sky/heaven is arched and vaulted, see *Embracing the Circle: Domical Buildings in East Asian Architecture ca. 200–750*, 17–19.

34 Sun Zongwen, *Zhongguo jianzhu yu zhexue* (Nanjing, 2000), 95–98.

Yet according to modern architect and scholar Li Yunhe, the term *liu* also referred to a special roof structure related to primitive hut. Through stacking either square or polygonal wooden frames, one after another, each layer of the structure is smaller than the one below. By doing this, a roof structure is formed in a tapered shape that does not need columnar support. At the very top of the roof structure, a skylight would be formed by the smallest square or polygon frame (see Figure 2). Li also believes that the construction of *liu* later developed into a distinctive tectonic component within a building, that is, the *zaojing*.[35]

There are two qualities of *zhongliu* which make it the architype of *zaojing*—one is its central location directly opening to the sky, and the other is its inherent association with flowing water, like an inverted water well. The Qing scholar Li Dou 李斗 first articulated the connection between *zhongliu* and *zaojing* in his architectural treatise *Gongduan yingzao lu* 工段营造录. As Li stated, "in ancient times, [an opening] on the wall is called *you* 牖, and that on the top of a room is called *chuang* 囱 or 窗."[36] Clearly, Li was referring to the very meaning of "chuang" (囱, or 窗) stipulated in the Han lexicon *Shuowen jiezi*.[37] It should be noted that the character "囱" also pronounced as *cong*, means a chimney. The interchangeability between window and chimney, reflected by the same Chinese character "囱," reveals their combined functions in early times as *zhongliu*. To Li, *zaojing* originated from the skylight, and he added:

> *Liushu zhengyi* 六书正义 [a Ming dynasty book] indicates that fenestration forms *jiong* 冏 [brightness, by pictorially showing an opening in a room], whose shape is like a square well inversely hanging down from the rooftop. It is decorated with a floral motif, with roots up and foliage down. A lantern is often placed inside the fenestration shimmering like a pearl. This fenestration is called a skylight.[38]

Similarly, Li Yunhe believes that some early Chinese pictographs truthfully reflect architectural forms. Taking the character of "窗" *chuang* (window) for example, the upper component (穴, *xue*) suggests a cave and the lower

35 Li Yunhe, *Cathay's Idea: Design Theory of Chinese Classical Architecture* (Tianjin, 2013), 206.
36 Li Dou, *Gongduan yingzao lu* (Beijing, 2009), unpaginated.
37 *Shuowen jiezi zhu*, 490.
38 Li, *Gongduan yingzao lu*.

component (囪, *chuang*) is an opening. This indicates that the origin of window was derived from a skylight in a primitive cave.[39] The character "囪" *chuang* itself was a pictograph. According to *Shuowen jiezi*, the small seal script of *chuang* expressively indicated a pattern that was formed by wooden battens crossing each other (Figure 3.11).[40]

The architectural detail of an aperture can be found in numerous pottery models and stone reliefs from the Han period (Figure 3.12). If such a window was placed on the ceiling, then it formed a skylight and could be called as *zaojing*. For example, in the Han tomb at Beizhai village, there are a number of *zaojing* that directly borrowed the form of a window without any alteration (Figures 3.13 and 3.14).

Though developing the window architype, in Han architecture, *zaojing* was a symbolic element and consequently did not have to follow the pattern

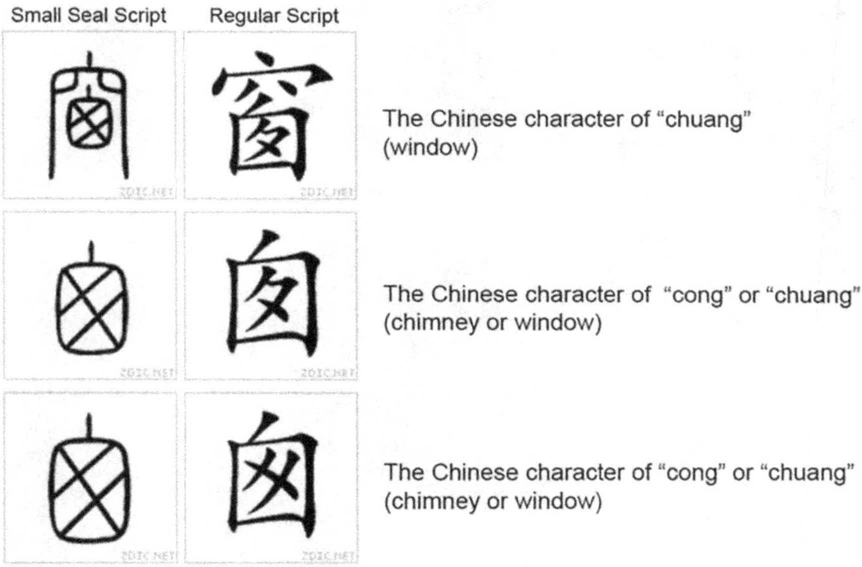

Figure 3.11 The transformation of the characters *chuang* 窗 and *cong* 囱, 囪, originally they were all referring to an opening of a room, in *Han Dian*, http://www.zdic.net/z/20/zy/7A97.htm; http://www.zdic.net/z/17/zy/56EA.htm; http://www.zdic.net/z/17/zy/56F1.htm (access April 26, 2018).

39 Li, *Cathay's Idea*, 49.
40 *Shuowen jiezi zhu*, 490.

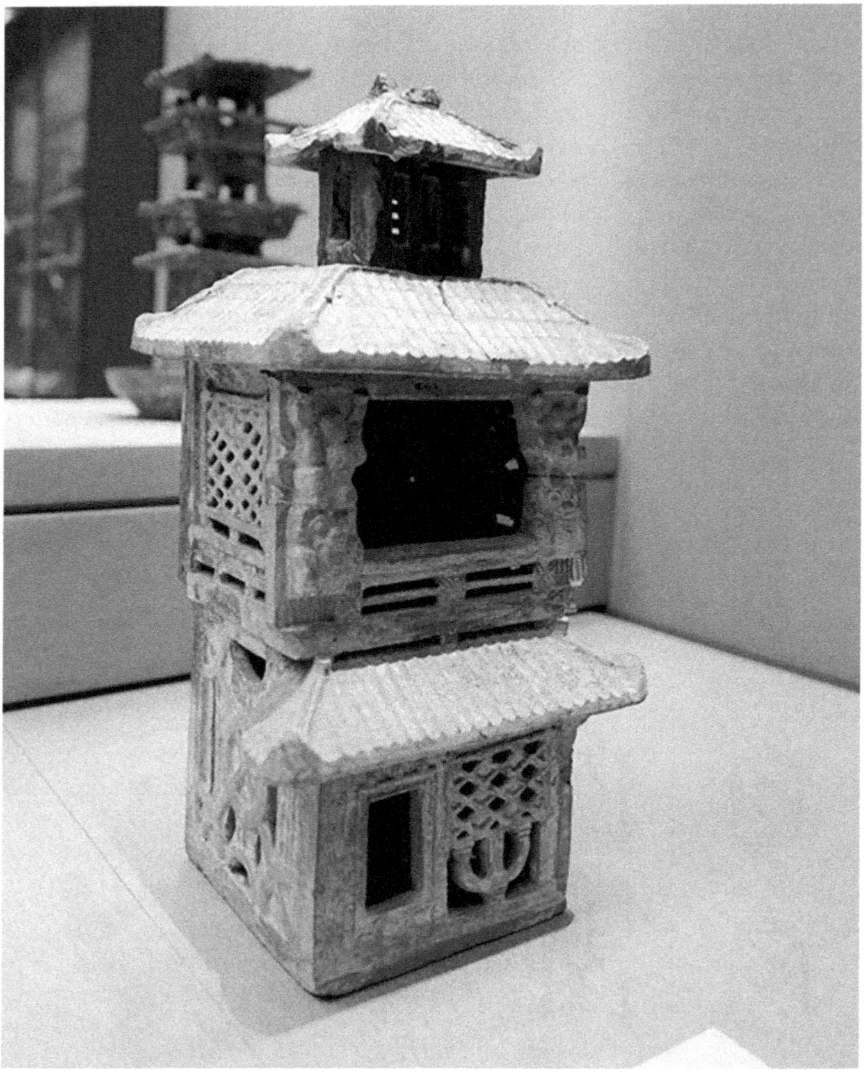

Figure 3.12 A pottery model of a pavilion, from the Eastern Han period, unearthed in Xiangcheng County, Henan Province (Henan Museum, author's photo, 2021).

of densely crossing battens typical of a window, since the purpose of these was to block access, visually and physically. As widely evidenced, a pattern consisting of one diamond shape within a square frame was sufficient to reflect the common expression of *zaojing*, indicating its early association with a window (see Figures 2 and 3.15).

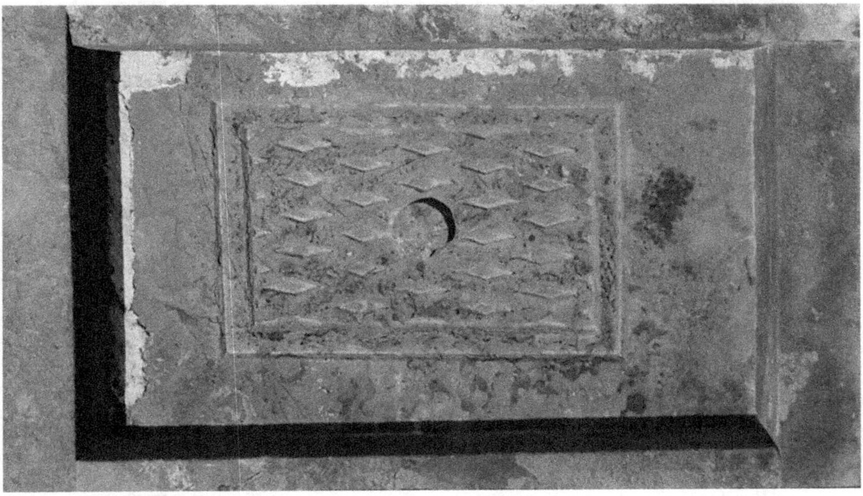

Figure 3.13 *Zaojing* in the western wing room of the central chamber in the Beizhai tomb (author's photo, 2022).

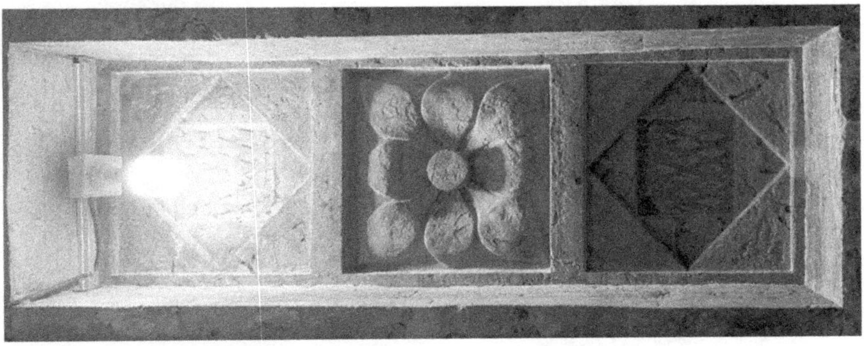

Figure 3.14 *Zaojing* in the back chamber of the Beizhai tomb (author's photo, 2022).

Zaojing and the Constellations

In many cases from the Han dynasty, *zaojing* were built on a more elaborate pattern, for example, three squares concentrically organized with the middle one rotated by 45 degrees, all swirling up toward the sky (Figure 3.15). To further articulate the privilege of *zaojing*, a circle was inserted in the middle of *zaojing* in some cases (Figure 3.16). Painted in red and with a black bird in the center, the circle symbolized the sun (Figure 3.17). In this sense, *zaojing* was still a skylight such that when the sun was shining its connection to celestial bodies was pronounced.

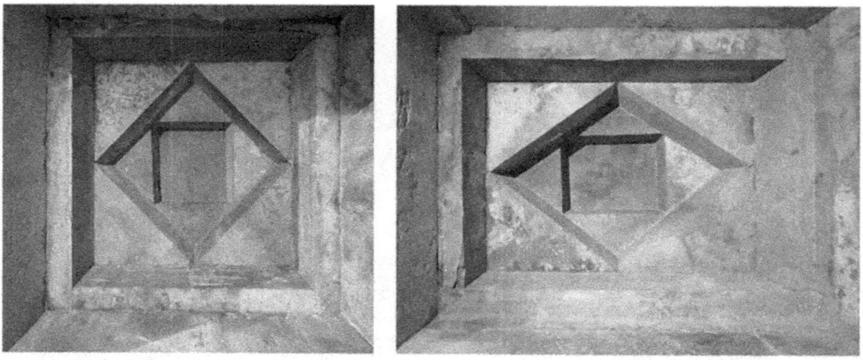

Figure 3.15 *Zaojing* in the eastern and western wing rooms of the front chamber in the Beizhai tomb (author's photo, 2022).

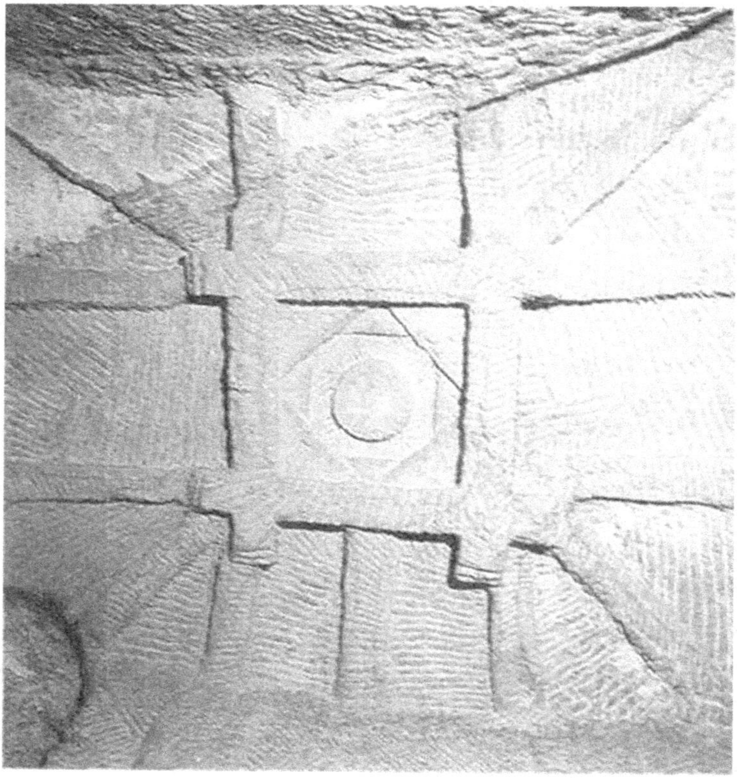

Figure 3.16 Stone *zaojing* in the right-wing room of the front chamber, from the Han tomb Dongzipai No. 1 in Santai County, Sichuan Province (source: *Kaogu*, 1 (2002), 32, fig. 39).

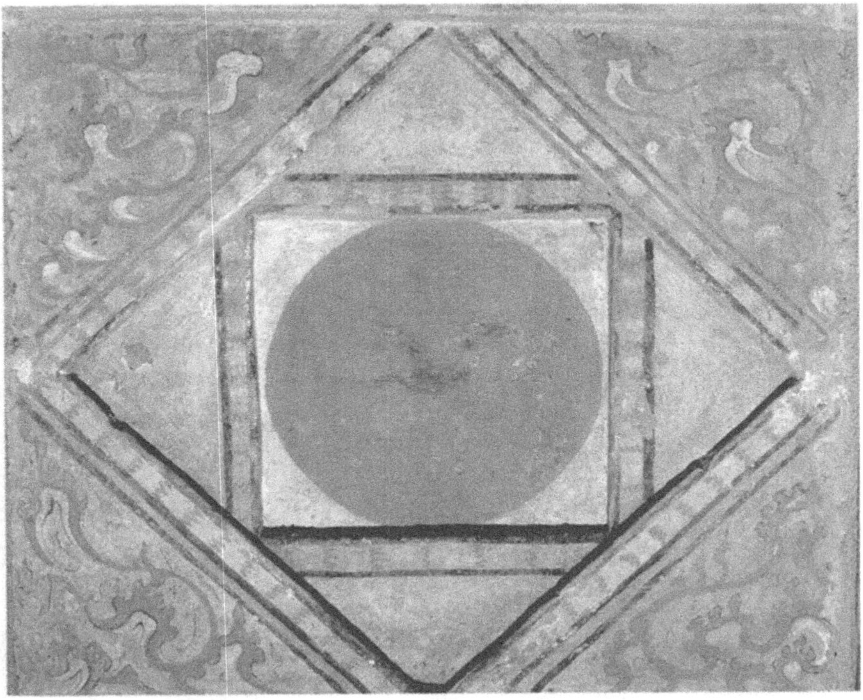

Figure 3.17 *Zaojing* with the sun on the ridge of the back chamber, as a mural, from the tomb of the Xin dynasty (9–23) at Jianguyuan, Luoyang, Henan Province (source: Huang Minglan and Guo Yinqiang, eds., *Luoyang Han mu bihua* (Beijing, 1996), 111, fig. 4).

Longing for heaven became an extremely popular theme in Han society.[41] In the belief that heavenly order had an inherent value to the social and political lives on earth, as discussed in Chapter 2, cosmology from earlier times, such as astrology and *wuxing*, was further developed in the Han dynasty to guide political life and to consolidate imperial sovereignty as the Mandate of Heaven. It was in the process of establishing Han cosmology and its worldview that *zaojing* had acquired a new connotation.

Since the Western Han dynasty, a unique political and cultural practice for fire protection had been developed in the court that once a major fire incident happened, the emperor would issue a decree confessing his own guilt (i.e., 罪己诏,

41 Lillian Lan-ying Tseng, *Picturing Heaven in Early China* (Cambridge, MA, 2011).

zuiji zhao). As the Son of Heaven, the emperor was fully responsible for punishment from heaven.[42] A number of architectural methods for fire control were adopted, such as building fire compartment walls and spaces to separate buildings and providing water reservoirs near to buildings. Yet the most unique solution for fire protection was the introduction of *zaojing*, a special ceiling treatment that was further crafted based on the motif of the water well. *Zao* 藻 means algae, referring to aquatic plants. *Jing* 井, means a well. Fitting into the conquest cycle of *wuxing* in which Water conquers Fire by extinguishing it, *zaojing* is striving to represent a theme of water. Physically, it was impossible to make an inverted water well which actually contained water. The architectural metaphor thus was adopted to adorn *zaojing* with hydrophyte plants that implied the existence of water.

The literature accounts of *zaojing* from the Han dynasty were abundant enough to create a vivid picture. In *Xijingfu* 西京赋 (*Western Metropolis Rhapsody*), written by the renowned Han astronomer and scholar Zhang Heng 张衡, the great hall in the imperial palace had "rooted inverted lotus stalks on the *zaojing*, which bloomed with red flowers joining one another."[43] Similarly, *zaojing* in the Hall of Numinous Brilliance was portrayed as:

> a round pool on the square well, in which lotus flowers were inverted. They were bursting with florescence, erupting in bloom, their blossoms spread and open, their green pods and purple fruit bulging and bloated like dangling pearls.[44]

Such architectural rhetoric can also be confirmed by the *zaojing* from Han tombs. For example, in the back chamber of the Beizhai tomb, the ceiling consists of three *zaojing*. The central *zaojing* is a lotus flower with eight petals (see Figure 3.14).

It was in *Fengsu tongyi* 风俗通义 (a book of folk customs in the Han dynasty) that the role of *zaojing* for suppressing fire was advanced. As it stated, "the great halls often contain the form of Dongjing 东井, where lotus and water chestnuts were carved. As these plants are hydrophytic, they suppress fire."[45]

---

42 Li Caiqi, *Zhongguo xiaofang wenshi zongtan* (Shanghai, 2013), 70–74.

43 Zhang Heng, "*Xijing fu*," in *Zhaoming Wen Xuan*, 37–67. The English translation by Knechtges, *Wen Xuan or Selections of Refined Literature, Volume I*, 187–189. The translation is slightly modified by the author.

44 Wang Yanshou, "*Lu Lingguang dian fu*," in *Zhaoming Wen Xuan*, 324–335. The English translation by Knechtges, *Wen Xuan or Selections of Refined Literature, Volume II*, 271. The translation is slightly modified by the author.

45 Ying Shao, *Fengsu tongyi jiaozhu* (Beijing, 2015), 575.

Dongjing was the name of the constellation, which was also known as Jingxiu 井宿. By linking the architectural feature *zaojing* to the form of Dongjing, the text uplifted the connotation of *zaojing* from a water well to the constellation.

Sima Qian stated that "Dongjing is the constellation in charge of water affairs."[46] In order to verify the role of Dongjing regarding water affairs, all the surrounding constellations were also named with a water theme in the Han period. Connected with Dongjing, there were other constellations named as follows: Nanhe 南河 (South River), Beihe 北河 (North River), Jishui 积水 (Stored Water), Shuiwei 水位 (Water Level), Sidu 四渎 (Four Rivers), and Shuifu 水府 (Water Palace). As Sun Xiaochun and Jacob Kistemaker stated, one can easily observe that Dongjing is located just to the east of the Celestial River—the Milky Way—and is portrayed as a general picture of water and rivers.[47] Sima also asserted that "at the time when the Han dynasty was thriving, an astronomical phenomenon occurred with the five solar planets assembled in Dongjing."[48] This indicated the importance of Dongjing as an auspicious constellation, in assuring a prosperous life for the dynasty.

The pattern of the Dongjing constellation reflects the Chinese character of *jing* (Figure 3.18). The point of establishing a close link between *zaojing* and Dongjing is understandable: if *zaojing* is referring merely to an ordinary well, then it lacks magical power to suppress fire. But Dongjing is different. It is a celestial body also supported by other constellations. The concept of bringing down celestial water in suppressing terrestrial fire is also tangible in a number of Han pottery models of wells.[49] One Han pottery well excavated at Yanshi County, Henan Province, for example, shows that the character of *jing* is underlined by the cap frame of the well balustrade (Figure 3.19). The structure of the windlass is installed on the top of the well. Most importantly, there are four Chinese characters carved on the balustrade "Dongjing miehuo 东井灭火," meaning the constellation of Dongjing suppresses fire.[50] From these Han pottery wells, we see that a well plays an essential role in daily life at that time, and by their carved text indicating the role of Dongjing, a connection between heaven and earth is emphatically underlined.

46 Sima Qian, *Shiji*, vol. 1, 479.

47 Sun Xiaochun and Jacob Kistemaker, *The Chinese Sky during the Han: Constellating Stars and Society* (Leiden, 1997), 119.

48 Sima, *Shiji*, vol. 1, 495.

49 Xiong Long, "Textual research on the wordings 'Dongjing jiehuo' of pottery wells," *Wenbo*, 01 (2012): 38–44.

50 See ibid and Wei Qiuping, "Supplementary textual research on 'Dongjing jiehuo' of pottery wells and reliefs," *Wenbo*, 04 (2013): 46–49.

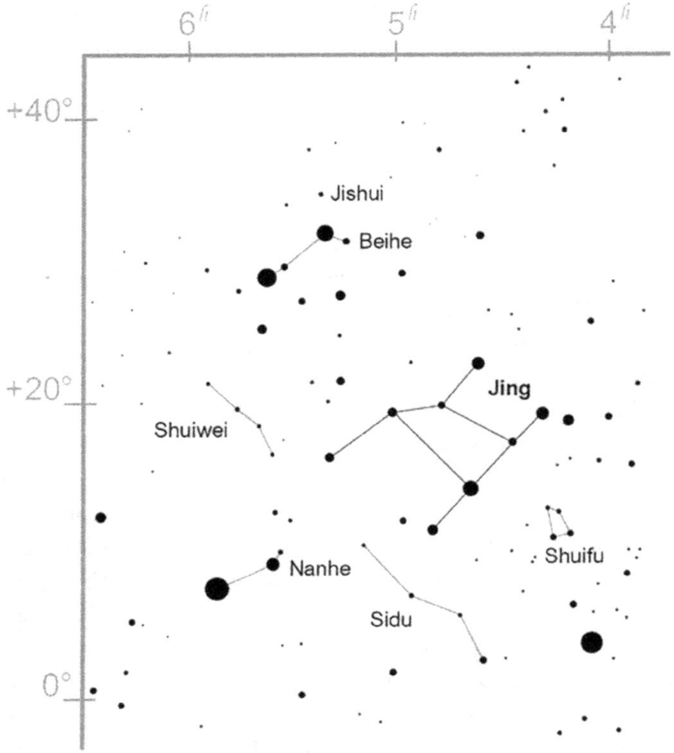

Figure 3.18 Marked as "Jing," Dongjing in the Han sky (author's drawing, 2019, based on Sun and Kistemaker, *The Chinese Sky during the Han*, 139, fig. 6.9).

Mystical Quality of *Zaojing*

In parallel to the development of a well (or *zaojing*) from an astronomical perspective, water wells were also endowed with magical power in early China. Far beyond being a daily necessity for providing a water source, a well was often regarded as a celestial creation. *Shanhai jing* 山海经, for example, was a book completed in the early Han dynasty with much of the content produced in the fourth century BCE, illustrated many water wells sitting among natural landscapes. The book recorded, in the southern area of Chao Mountain, a well that contained water in the winter but became dry in the summer.[51] Similarly, on the top of Shi Mountain, there is a well named

51 *Shanhai jing yizhu* (Shanghai, 2014), 171.

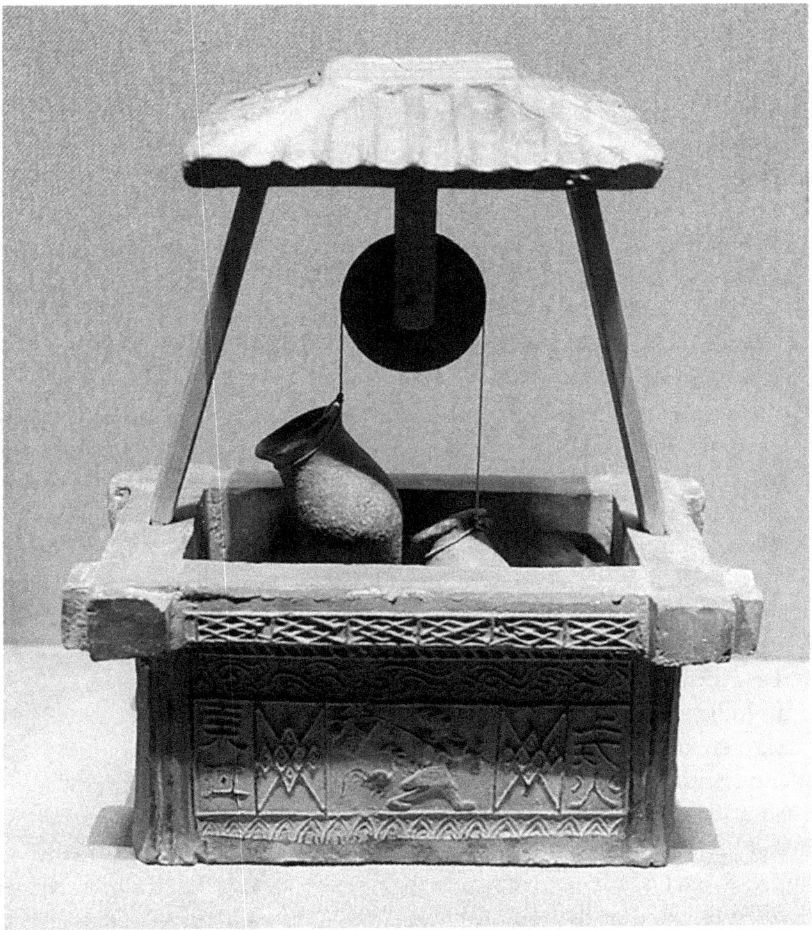

Figure 3.19 A grey pottery model of a water well from the early Eastern Han period, unearthed in Yanshi County, Henan Province (Henan Museum, author's photo, 2021).

tianjing (sky well) that contains water in the summer and dries in the winter.[52] Moreover, in Kunlun Mountain, the legendary place associated with heaven and gods, there are nine wells whose elevated frames are made from jade.[53]

Hanshu 汉书 also recorded the supernatural phenomena associated with wells in its categorization of *wuxing* and used the theory of Five Elements to interpret these phenomena. For example, in 193 BCE, there were two live

52 Ibid., 223.
53 Ibid., 294.

dragons that appeared in a water well located in an urban neighborhood. To the Han scholar Liu Xiang 刘向, the dragons symbolized nobility, yet they were now stranded in a commoner's well. This could be interpreted as an ill omen of the possible imprisonment of dukes or princes.[54] The same story was also recorded in another mythological book *Soushen ji* 搜神记, written by Gan Bao 干宝 in the Jin dynasty (265–420).[55] This historic account might well reveal an opposite scenario, that is, as a celestial creature, a dragon should be living in the sky. As an architectural representation, *zaojing* could be regarded as a water well in the sky. If there was a carved or painted dragon appearing on *zaojing*, this would indicate an auspicious omen. Indeed, *zaojing* with the dragon motif prevailed in important buildings throughout late imperial China (see Figure 3).

Water wells in the mountains also contributed to the Taoist practice of pursuing immortality. In the mythological/historical book *Shiyi ji* 拾遗记, compiled by the Taoist scholar Wang Jia 王嘉 during the Jin dynasty, the illustration of wells, in terms of their magical character, appears even more vivid than ever before. For example, in the reign of the Yan Emperor, the legendary Chinese ruler in pre-dynastic times, there was a mountain named Junhuan 峻锾. At the foot of the mountain, there was a golden well whose top was cloaked in white mist. The gold inside the well was very soft and could easily be bound or twisted by hand.[56] It should be noted that gold was an indispensable metal element for the Taoist practice of alchemy. In 265, a foreign envoy came to the Wei court describing a well in his country, which was built with red stones and was definitely beyond the capacity of human craftsmanship. Connected to a secret spring below, the well often gushed with water. This well not only offered drinking water but also a special cuisine to immortals, that is, a species of white frog with two wings that lived in the water and often lingered at the top of the well.[57] Questioned by the scholar-official Zhang Hua 张华 (232–300), the envoy's account seemed to be hardly worthy of belief, yet it must have been appealing to Taoists or it would not have been included in Wang's treatise.[58]

Although as mysterious as these literary accounts of wells sound, there is an inherent relationship between earth and heaven that can be manifested by wells. This is articulated by Sun Zongwen through examining the text

54 Ban Gu, *Hanshu*, 202.
55 Gan Bao, *Soushen ji* (Beijing, 1985), 72.
56 Wang Jia, *Shiyi ji* (Beijing, 1988), 5.
57 Ibid., 209.
58 Ibid.

concerning wells from the imperial period.[59] As acknowledged in early China, building a well was to liberate underground springs that were the veins of the earth, that is, supernatural ley lines. The movement of underground water was determined by the constellations, which, in simple terms, was clearly demonstrated by the movement of the moon and its impact on water levels on the earth. Hence, the location for digging a water well should be carefully considered with the aid of astronomy.[60]

Such a strong vertical connection established between wells and heaven certainly had a long-lasting influence on the development of *zaojing*. In particular, the Han concept of water well and *zaojing* left its indelible imprint on the development of Buddhist caves that commenced in China in the fourth century. Taking the most famous one, Mogao Caves in Dunhuang, Gansu Province whose construction spanned nine centuries continuously, are indeed a treasure trove offering more than 400 caves that contain different patterns of *zaojing*. Taking Cave No. 249 as an example, built in the Western Wei period (535–557), its *zaojing* witnesses the fusion of Buddhist and Chinese worldviews at that time (Figure 3.20). The whole ceiling is in an upside-down ladle shape with a square *zaojing* on the very top and four sloping sides connecting to the walls. In fact many ceiling forms of Mogao Caves are termed *fudou* 覆斗 or *daodou* 倒斗, suggesting a large inverted *dou* form, which also reveals a close connection between *zaojing* and *dougong*.[61] The *zaojing* consists of three squares concentrically organized and rotated by 45 degrees. In the center, there is a circular lotus surrounded by a foliage pattern. The four slopes were painted with celestial motifs: the west is the Buddhist god Asura, the east is Mani Jewel, the north is Dongwanggong 东王公 (King Father of the East, a popular god in the Han dynasty), and the south is Xiwangmu 西王母 (Queen Mother of the West, a popular goddess in the Han dynasty). They are all surrounded by celestial figures and creatures, expressing the combined cosmic views of Buddhism and the Han Chinese.[62]

Considering the original functions of *zaojing* discussed earlier, that is, for illumination, ventilation, and worship, it seemed to be a fitting solution to adopt *zaojing* in Buddhist caves. In a symbolic manner, *zaojing* introduced celestial light into the dark caves. As the most important element in a human

59 Sun, *Zhongguo jianzhu yu zhexue*, 100–103.

60 Ibid.

61 Xiao Mo, *Dunhuang jianzhu yanjiu* (Beijing, 2019), 385–394.

62 The Editorial Committee of the complete murals in Dunhuang, ed., *Zhongguo Dunhuang bihua quanji, Western Wei* (Tianjin, 2002), vol. 2, 29. Jun Hu has also discussed Cave No. 249, see *Embracing the Circle*, 54–63.

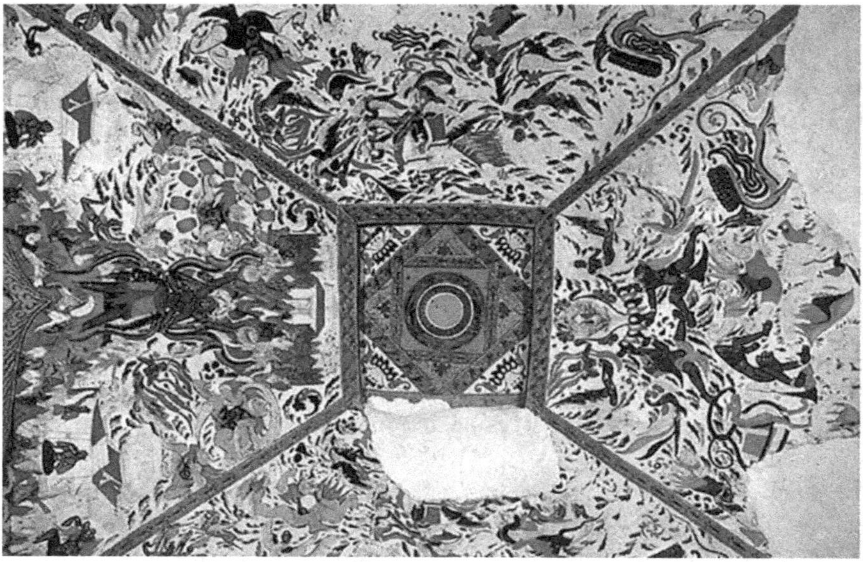

Figure 3.20 The ceiling and *zaojing* in the no. 249 cave of Mogao Caves, built in the Western Wei period (535–557) (source: The Editorial Committee of the complete murals in Dunhuang, ed., *Zhongguo Dunhuang bihua quanji, Western Wei,* vol. 2, 29, fig. 61).

dwelling associated with worship (i.e., *zhongliu*, the architype of *zaojing* discussed earlier), *zaojing* might naturally be included in Buddhist caves as an expression of reverence. More importantly, dedicated to Buddhism, *zaojing* in Mogao Caves emphasized the vertical struggle involved in ascending to heaven.

Zaojing in Succeeding Dynasties

Although the stone and painted *zaojing* flourished in Buddhist caves during the Tang dynasty, there are neither physical remains of *zaojing* in timber architecture nor much literature regarding *zaojing* from that period. This is most likely due to the relatively exclusive use of *zaojing* for elite architecture. Stated in *Xin Tangshu* 新唐书, Tang dukes and prices were not allowed to construct *chonggong* and *zaojing* in their houses.[63] This was a further restriction of sumptuary law compared to that recorded in *Tang huiyao* 唐会要.[64]

63 Ouyang Xiu and Song Qi, *Xin Tangshu* (Beijing, 1975), 532.
64 Wang Pu, *Tang huiyao* (Beijing, 1955), ch. 31, 575.

Interestingly, these two accounts were provided by the scholars in the succeeding dynasty. There was a renewed interest among the Song literati in reviewing and editing the classical texts from earlier periods, rejecting superstitious and mystical elements from Taoism and Buddhism. This formed the Neo-Confucianism movement that reached its peak in the Song period.

The Song understanding of *zaojing* is manifested in the classical construction manual *Yingzao fashi*, in which the scholar-official Li Jie 李诫 (1035–1110) dutifully listed the early literary accounts of *zaojing* and provided detailed construction methods and dimensions for three different types. Although Li cited the account from *Fengsu tongyi* that connected *zaojing* to the constellation Dongjing, he refrained from commentary but elaborated on the technical aspects of how to build *zaojing*.[65]

The astrological portents from preceding dynasties were also scrutinized and reinterpreted by the Song literati. For example, the Southern Song scholar Zheng Qiao 郑樵 (1104–1162) wrote extensively about astronomy based on an early text *Butian ge* 步天歌 arguably from the Sui-Tang period (581–907), which introduced the constellations by means of poetry.[66] *Butian ge* portrayed the constellation Dongjing as: "the eight stars laying across the Milky Way tranquilly 八星横列河中静."[67] Although it was much easier to understand the constellations in the form of poetry than in the literature of astronomy, there was a restriction on disseminating such poetry among the public in imperial China. As Zheng pointed out, *Butian ge* was only circulated within the Spirit Terraces (灵台, astronomical observatories).[68] Zheng also explicitly mentioned that Dongjing was also named *tianjing*, that is, sky well.[69]

Neither Zheng Qiao nor Li Jie, however, had articulated the connection between *zaojing* and the constellation Dongjing. *Douba zaojing* 斗八藻井 was the very term registered in *Yingzao fashi*, explained by Li as follows:

> there used to be three names [for *zaojing*]: the first one was "zaojing," the second was "circular spring 圆泉," and the third was "square well 方井." Today they are all called "douba zaojing."[70]

65 Li Jie, *Yingzao fashi* (Beijing, 2011), 15, 61–63.
66 Zheng Qiao, *Tongzhi lue* (Shanghai, 1990), 197.
67 Ibid., 206.
68 Ibid., 197.
69 Ibid., 206.
70 Li, *Yingzao fashi*, 61.

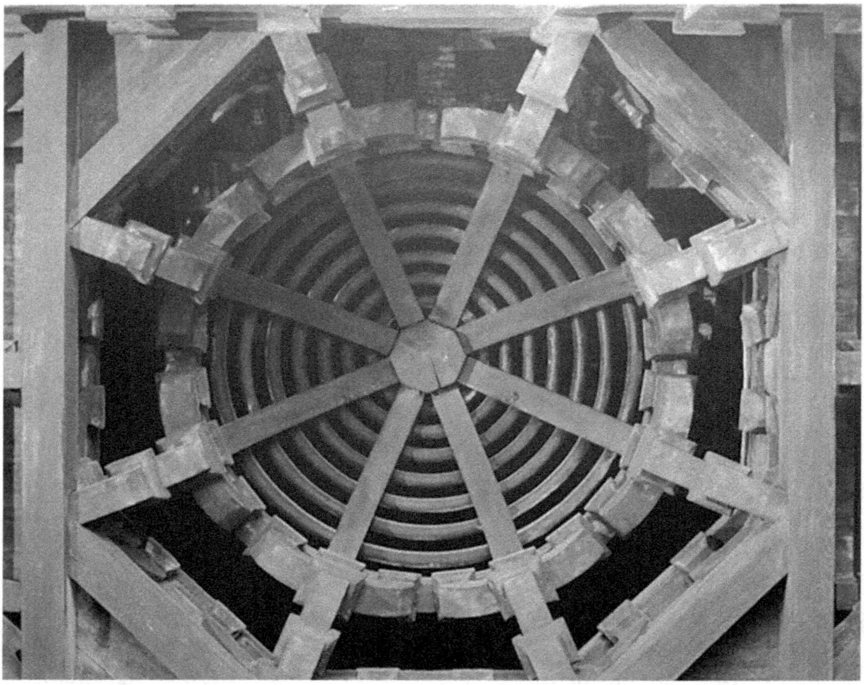

Figure 3.21 The central *zaojing* in the great hall of Baoguo Temple, built in 1013, Ningbo, Zhejiang Province (photo courtesy of Baoguosi Museum of Ancient Architecture).

To offer a clear picture of *zaojing* as stipulated in *Yingzao fashi*, we may turn to a relic of *zaojing* that remains in the great hall of Baoguo Temple in Ningbo, Zhejiang Province, built in 1013. As an example, par excellence, of *douba zaojing*, the central *zaojing* in the great hall of Baoguo Temple was elaborately constructed with eight wooden arched ribs, joining at the top octagonal block and extending to the eight *dougong* (bracket sets) at the bottom. Round sub-ribs were applied forming circles connecting the eight arched ribs, thereby articulating a domelike structure (Figure 3.21). This part, according to *Yingzao fashi*, was termed an "octagonal well."[71] The eight *dougong* were the key structure component holding up the octagonal well, therefore explaining the use of the term *douba* (i.e., eight blocks).

71 Ibid., 62.

In fact, the term *dou* 斗 was closely associated with the constellation Northern Dipper in the Han dynasty.[72] This association was soundly acknowledged in the Qing dynasty when the first history of Baoguo Temple was written:

> the great hall was rebuilt in 1013, with a unique structural system including cantilevers 昂, bracket arms 拱, and star-like blocks 星斗 that resulted in the most superb temple in the prefecture of Mingzhou [now Ningbo].[73]

Comparing the diagram of the constellation Dongjing, the character of *jing*, and the central *zaojing* in the great hall of Baoguo Temple, there is an inherent connection in the physical configurations (Figure 3.22). The term "*douba* 斗八" frequently appearing in *Yingzao fashi* was interchangeably used as *zaojing*, as the very word *douba* (eight blocks) implied eight stars, that is, the constellation of Dongjing.

Evident in many remaining historical buildings, there was a noticeable improvement in the craftsmanship of *zaojing* during the Ming–Qing dynasties (1368–1912). This is reflected in the complexity of their structures, variety of their physical forms, and the polychromy of their surface paintings. According to Li Yunhe, during the Ming–Qing period, a mirror was often placed in the center of a *zaojing*, symbolizing a skylight.[74] This practice was well recorded earlier in *Yingzao fashi* for the detailed construction of *douba zaojing*.[75] At the outset, a dragon was often painted in the mirror. In the Qing dynasty (1644–1912), the dragon motif in *zaojing* was further developed into a carved sculpture form (see Figure 3). Also, *zaojing* was commonly termed *longjing* 龙井 (dragon well).[76] No longer confined to imperial and religious buildings, *zaojing* also appeared in many theatre buildings, serving for a wide range of audiences (see Figure 4).

Liang Sicheng observed a trend of the development of *zaojing* in the Yuan, Ming, and Qing dynasties that it demonstrated a more refined and subtle taste than ever before. Remarkably, there was little literature about *zaojing*.

---

72 As discussed in the previous chapter; Similar comments from Pankenier, *Astrology and Cosmology in Early China*, 104.

73 Ming'an, ed, *Baoguo si zhi* (the collection of the temple, 1805). *Baoguo si zhi* is published together with the research project done by Guo Daiheng and her team, see Guo Daiheng and The Cultural Relics Preservation and Management Institute of Baoguo Temple, *Donglai diyi shan: Baoguo si* (Beijing, 2003).

74 Li, *Cathay's Idea*, 286.

75 Li, *Yingzao fashi*, 62.

76 Li, *Cathay's Idea*, 286.

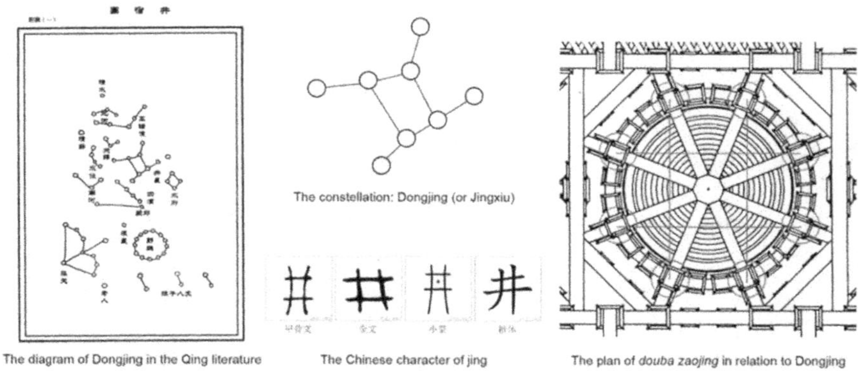

Figure 3.22 The diagram of Dongjing (or Jingxiu), from Hu Dianyu [Qing], *Qing Qianlong Ningyuan xian zhi xulue* (Lanzhou, 2005), 6. The character of *jing*, in *Han Dian*, http://www.zdic.net/z/15/zy/4E95.htm (access April 21, 2017). The projection plan of the central *douba zaojing* in the great hall of Baoguo Temple, with the eight *dougong* denoting the eight stars of Dongjing (author's drawing, 2017).

Even in the Qing official architecture treatise *Gongbu gongcheng zuofa zeli* 工部工程做法则例 (1734), the term *longjing* is only briefly mentioned without any explanation.[77] This probably verifies the modern theory that architecture itself is an effective text. Indeed, the imperial ideology of the cosmos was clearly manifested by the exquisite craftsmanship of *zaojing*.

Architectural Preservation in Modern Times

By the early twentieth century, the significance of *zaojing* was lost, as the discourse on architecture in China started to embrace ideas of the modern era, heavily influenced by Western culture. Along with development in technology, the belief that *zaojing* could suppress fire became mere superstition. There was no necessity for using *zaojing* to articulate social hierarchy. *Zaojing* appear in many modern governmental and cultural buildings, in a much more modest guise, as a decorative theme serving merely as a cultural symbol. Interestingly, no matter whether coffered, decorated, or flat, ceilings in China are commonly called *tianhua* 天花, a term derived in the Qing dynasty referring to a particular *zaojing* with a chessboard pattern.[78] Literally meaning sky flower, *tianhua* has figuratively captured one essence of *zaojing*.

77 Liang Sicheng and Liu Zhiping, "Zaojing Tianhua jianshuo," in: *Liang Sicheng quanji* (Beijing, 2001), VI, 416.
78 Ibid., 420.

In the preservation of historic buildings, modern means of fire protection were employed. For example, a common practice that started in modern Japan would be to install water pipes, smoke detectors, and sprinklers in historic structures, which would immediately cover a temple complex with water once a fire occurred. This solution was envied by Liang Sicheng, the famous Western-trained Chinese architect, who also hoped that one day China would catch up.[79] Well versed in premodern Chinese architecture, and in the manner of structural rationalism, Liang revived the *spirit* of Chinese great halls in the National Central Museum (completed in 1948). Originally, the design of the central part of the museum contained an octagonal *zaojing*.[80] Yet in the quest for modernity, or in other words, "to justify Chinese architecture in the modern era," the final solution was a simple hip roof resting on the bracket sets, beams, and lintels, supported by steel trusses concealed by the ceiling.[81] Even the *dougong* system was built in reinforced concrete.[82] Indeed, some modern building materials such as reinforced concrete will easily solve the fire problem.

In the case of the historic preservation of Baoguo Temple, almost all available cutting-edge technologies, such as lightning protection, a fire alarm system, sprinklers, a building information system, and wireless monitoring sensors, are all adopted to offer effective protection, assuring us that the great hall remain intact as the original structure.[83] Equipped with advanced computer monitors, sensors, and software, the structure is kept under constant surveillance. To use the official analogy, the historic structure is undergoing continuous "computer tomographic scanning," therefore sufficient data will be generated to make a correct diagnosis.[84]

By contrast, the premodern Chinese were unable to treat historic structures as if they were a moribund patient and scientifically diagnose them using advanced technology. The collapse or decay of buildings was seen as a natural cycle, often counterbalanced by rebuilding or renovating. In such a process, the architectural craftsmanship and knowledge overrode the physical form. Yet, more than a virtuosic display of craftsmanship,

79 Liang Sicheng, *Chinese Architecture: Art and Artifacts* (Beijing, 2013), 219.

80 Delin Lai, "Idealizing a Chinese Style: Rethinking Early Writings on Chinese Architecture and the Design of the National Central Museum in Nanjing," *Journal of the Society of Architectural Historians*, 73, no. 1 (March 2014): 72.

81 Ibid., 72, 76.

82 Ibid., 81, 86.

83 Baoguosi Museum of Ancient Architecture, ed, *Baoguo si xinzhi* (Beijing, 2013), 38–50, 260–274.

84 Ibid., 61.

Chinese traditional architecture was a symbolic space embodying the cosmic and political views of the elites. The construction of capital cities and major architecture had a noble intent, that is, to bring heavenly order down to guide human society.

Astrological analogy in major architecture also reflected an ideal Chinese order, that was, to Yi-Fu Tuan, "a deeply moral aesthetic."[85] Like Gothic cathedrals, though much less grand in scale, the great halls in China were also built in a tremendous effort to establish a dialogue with heaven. The wooden components of a building, including *zaojing* and bracket sets, columns and beams, windows and doors, and their elaborate and yet intriguing connections, were an ingenious achievement of craftsmanship and culture. The high-class joinery involved intricate mortise and tenon joints to hold different parts together such as the great hall of Baoguo Temple, much praised for not using any adhesives or fasteners during the construction. In addition, there were layers of decorative patterns and colored paintings. By their form, color, number, symbolism, and metaphor, all these architectural elements, as a complex whole, mirrored a harmonious universe. As in all religious architecture, there was a faith that human endeavor to create sublime architecture would reciprocally obtain divine blessings. If the aesthetic achievement in architecture still could not avert natural disasters such as fire, then the cause of the disaster must be moral corruption.

In the Three Kingdoms period (220–280), the great hall (崇华殿, Chonghua dian) in the palace of the state of Wei 魏 was destroyed by fire. Falling prey to panic, the emperor Cao Rui 曹叡 invited the court official Gao Tanglong 高堂隆 (?–237), an eminent scholar in planetary astrology, to discuss fire prevention. Facing a number of questions thrown by the emperor, such as "have I done something wrong?" and "Will building a larger palatial hall counteract evil forces?" Gao replied that the fires were an admonition from heaven. As long as the emperor obeyed the rules of etiquette and continuously improved his moral outlook, the fire disasters could be overcome. The belief that damaging influences could be counteracted simply by building extravagantly was however admonished by sages and men of moral virtue as a form of witchcraft.[86]

85 Yi-Fu Tuan, *Passing Strange and Wonderful: Aesthetics, Nature, and Culture* (Washington, DC, 1993), 191.

86 Chen Shou, *Sanguo zhi*, vol. 6, *Weishu*, vol. 6 (Chengdu, 2013), 1904.

This idea was addressed earlier by Sima Qian who ranked moral rectitude as the highest accomplishment of rulership. As Sima wrote:

> in all cases of celestial anomalies, if the [regular] measures are overstepped, then prognosticate [...] The ultimate superior cultivates virtue, the next level practices [good] government, the next level carries out relief efforts, the next level conducts sacrificial rituals, and below that nothing [is done].[87]

Through the study of the development of *zaojing*, we see that the prevention of fire in the past was imaginatively achieved with heavenly water. The effectiveness of such protection, first, lies in the exquisite craftsmanship that could artistically transform a wooden ceiling into a celestial world of water. Second, it lies in the religious belief that bringing down heavenly forces would assure safety, prosperity, and peace on earth. Last, but not the least, it lies in the moral axiom that virtue conquers everything. Interestingly, both the modern and the premodern efforts are driven by fear. The modern Chinese fear that the historic structure will collapse, leading to a devastating loss of valuable assets. The premodern Chinese, however, were not so obsessed with value, a very modern notion associated with money. Their fear was a "numinous dread," to use Rudolf Otto's words, that is, "to keep a thing holy in the heart."[88] Indeed, reverence for heaven was a driving force for the transformation of *zaojing* from earth to heaven. In establishing such a vertical connection to heaven, *zaojing*, as an architectural device, fundamentally implies the perfection of morality.

---

87 Pankenier, *Astrology and Cosmology in Early China*, 300; for the original Chinese text, see Sima, *Shiji*, vol. 1, 496.

88 Otto, *The Idea of the Holy*, 13–15.

EPILOGUE

As the two important elements in Chinese architecture, *dougong* and *zaojing* are beyond structural or functional necessity, and they are largely absent in most commoner's dwellings—the housing form for the majority in premodern China. Perhaps it is due to their lack of connection with basic needs or utilitarian architectural necessity that their cultural significance, as the connotation of transcendence, can be understood.

To attribute a transcendental quality to *dougong* and *zaojing* is because both are transformed from ordinary objects to something extraordinary. *Dou* in its original text means a ladle that is an everyday living utensil, and the term *zaojing* was derived from a water well that provided natural resources for daily life. In the process of transformation, arts played an essential role of adopting *dou* and *well* in important buildings, and then, within these small cosmoses, uplifting them to celestial bodies. The Chinese longing for heavens, also as a ruling social theme, is evident through the development of *dougong* and *zaojing*. As this book has demonstrated, the sources of inquiry extend far beyond architectural purview, involving scholarship in archaeology, philology, sociology, arts, and history. From such multidisciplinary perspectives, I hope that the connection between small architectural elements (i.e., *dougong* and *zaojing*) and broad Chinese cosmology can be revealed more fully.

As Chapter 1 has demonstrated, due to very limited textual record from the Shang-Zhou dynasties, pictorial patterns and physical forms of bronze vessels become the main source of inquiry. In these pieces of bronzes and associated ritual ceremonies, there is a strong religious struggle to establish a dialogue with the gods, searching for assurance and blessing. In response to the uncertain living environment, dictated by unforeseeable natural disasters or human wars, the bronze artifacts were solid and tangible, and served as an emotional anchor to the early Chinese in their unstable world. They had a close relation with their contemporaneous architecture too. In this sense, the scholarly claims that the Chinese did not intend to lodge their urban history in buildings, but rather in text as a form of accumulated memories, seems untrue.[1] Such claims can also be contested by numerous solid artifacts, such as stone tombs, reliefs, and pottery models, from the Han dynasty. As Chapter 2 indicates, both text and material objects flourished in the Han period, both expressing certain worldviews. In particular, the Chinese imagination of the heavens had most intense and diverse expressions, evident in the various motifs of columns and *dougong*. During the Spring and Autumn period as well as the Warring States period, early mythical and religious beliefs have been largely replaced by philosophies, namely the Hundred Schools of Thought, that flourished from the sixth century BCE to 221 BCE. Up to the Han dynasty, a more comprehensive cosmological view had been formed and it was also well integrated into court politics through the development of Confucianism. As Chapter 3 has illustrated, it is clear that aesthetics, moral philosophy, and politics were seamlessly integrated in the Han period, serving the common theme of connecting the heavens.

During the early intellectual development of religious beliefs, philosophies, and court politics, *dougong* and *zaojing* had played the role of art in architecture, presenting, to borrow Iris Murdoch's words, "the most comprehensible examples of the almost irresistible human tendency to seek consolation in fantasy."[2] The fantasy was based on the worldview of the early Chinese elites, that is, in essence, morality leads to immortality. Therefore, it would be absurd to view *dougong* and *zaojing* as redundant decorative elements from a modern perspective. It would also be regrettable if the physical forms of *dougong* and *zaojing* were creatively adopted to modern architectural practice without an awareness of the compelling themes that once resided in these two elements.

1 Many sinologists hold such a viewpoint, for example, Arthur F. Wright, "The Cosmology of the Chinese City," in: *The City in Late Imperial China*, ed., G. W. Skinner (Taipei, 1997), 33–37; F. W. Mote, "A Millennium of Chinese Urban History: Form, Time, and Space Concepts in Soochow," *The Rice University Studies*, vol. 59, no. 4, 1973, 35–65; Simon Leys, "The Chinese Attitude towards the past," in: *The Hall of Uselessness: Collected Essays* (New York, 2013), 285–301.

2 Iris Murdoch, *The Sovereignty of Good* (London, 1970), 62–63.

BIBLIOGRAPHY

Aurelius, Marcus. *Meditations* (Nanjing: Yilin chubanshe, 2016).

Ban Gu 班固 [32–92], *Hanshu* 汉书 [*Book of the Han*] (Xi'an: Taibai wenyi chubanshe, 2006).

Baoguosi Museum of Ancient Architecture 保国寺古建筑博物馆, ed., *Baoguo si xinzhi* 保国寺新志 [*New History of Baoguo Temple*] (Beijing: Wenwu chubanshe, 2013).

Bowu zhi (wai qi zhong) 博物志 (外七种) [*Records of Diverse Matters (And Seven Other Essays)*], ed., Wang Genlin 王根林 (Shanghai: Shanghai guji chubanshe, 2012).

Chang, K. C. 张光直, *Zhongguo qingtong shidai* 中国青铜时代 [*The Chinese Bronze Age*] (Beijing: Sanlian shudian, 1999).

———. *Art, Myth, and Ritual: The Path to Political Authority in Ancient China* (Cambridge, MA: Harvard University Press, 1983).

Chen Mengjia 陈梦家, *Xi Zhou tongqi duandai* 西周铜器断代 [*Historic Study of the Western Zhou Bronzes*] (Beijing: Zhonghua shuju, 2004).

Chen Mingda 陈明达, *Zhongguo gudai mujiegou jianzhu jishu: Zhanguo-Beisong* 中国古代木结构建筑技术: 战国-北宋 [*The Architectural Technology of Wooden Structures in Ancient China: From the Warring States to the Northern Song*] (Beijing: Wenwu chubanshe, 1990).

Chen Shou 陈寿 [233–297], *Sanguo zhi*, vol. 6, *Weishu*, vol. 6 三国志 6 魏书 6 (Chengdu: Bashu shushe, 2013).

Childs-Johnson, Elizabeth. "Urban daemons of early Shang: Urbanism in ancient China," *Archaeological Research in Asia*, vol. 14 (June 2018): 135–150.

Creel, Herrlee Glessner. *The Birth of China: A Survey of the Formative Period of Chinese Civilization* (London: Jonathan Cape Ltd., 1936).

Dai De 戴德 [Western Han], ed., *Da Dai Liji jinzhu jinyi* 大戴礼记今注今译 [*The Modern Annotated Records of Ritual Matters by Dai the Elder*], trans. Gao Ming 高明 (Tianjin: Tianjin guji chubanshe, 1975).

Dong Zhongshu 董仲舒 [179–104 BCE], *Chunqiu fanlu* 春秋繁露 [*Luxuriant Dew of the Spring and Autumn Annals*] (Zhengzhou: Zhongzhou guji chubanshe, 2010).

Dongfang Shuo 东方朔 [Western Han], *Shenyi jing* 神异经 [*Classic of Spirits and Oddities*], in *Bowu zhi (wai qi zhong)*, 85–100.

Du Jinpeng 杜金鹏, "Zhouyuan gongdian jianzhu leixing ji xiangguan wenti tantao 周原宫殿建筑类型及相关问题探讨 [A typological study of the palace buildings at Zhouyuan and related questions]," *Kaogu xuebao* 考古学报 [*Acta Archeologica Sinica*], vol. 4 (2009): 435–468.

Erya yizhu 尔雅译注 [*The Annotated Near Correctness*], eds., Hu Qiguang 胡奇光 and Fang Huanhai 方环海 (Shanghai: Shanghai guji chubanshe, 2012).

Fan Ye 范晔 [389–445], *Hou Hanshu* 后汉书 [*Book of the Later Han*] (Xi'an: Taibai wenyi chubanshe, 2006).

Feng, Jiren. *Chinese Architecture and Metaphor: Song Culture in the Yingzao Fashi Building Manual* (Honolulu: University of Hawai'i Press, 2012).

Fengxiang County Cultural Centre 凤翔县文化馆 and Shaanxi Provincial Committee for Management of Cultural and Historical Relics 陕西省文管会, "Fengxiang xian Qin gongdian shijue ji tongzhi jianzhu goujian 凤翔先秦宫殿试掘及其铜质建筑构件 [The excavation of pre-Qin palace building in Fengxiang site and the bronze architectural fittings]," *Kaogu* 考古 [*Archaeology*], no. 2 (1976): 121–132.

Fu Xinian 傅熹年, *Jianzhu shi lunwen xuan* 建筑史论文选 [*Collection of Papers in Architectural History*] (Tianjin: Baihua wenyi chubanshe, 2009).

Gan Bao 干宝 [?–336], *Soushen ji* 搜神记 [*In Search of the Supernatural*] (Beijing: Zhonghua shuju, 1985).

Gu Xiegang 顾颉刚, "zhongliu you fuxue lai 中霤由复穴来 [zhongliu derives from fuxue]," in: *Gu Xiegang quanji* 顾颉刚全集 24 [*Complete Writings of Gu Xiegang*] (Beijing: Zhonghua shuju, 2011), vol. 24.

———, *Shilin zashi* 史林杂识 (Beijing: Zhonghua shuju, 1963).

Guliang Chi 穀梁赤 [Zhou], *Chunqiu Guliang zhuan zhushu* 春秋穀梁传注疏, annotated by Fan Ning 范宁 [Jin] and Yang Shixun 杨士勋 [Tang] (printed in the Qing dynasty).

Guo Daiheng 郭黛姮 and The Cultural Relics Preservation and Management Institute of Baoguo Temple 宁波保国寺文物保管所, *Donglai diyi shan: Baoguo si* 东来第一山:保国寺 [*The First Mountain from the East: Baoguo Temple*] (Beijing: Wenwu chubanshe, 2003).

Guo Huayu 郭华瑜, *Zhongguo gudian jianzhu xingzhi yuanliu* 中国古典建筑形制源流 [*The Origin and Development of Classical Chinese Architectural Forms*] (Wuhan: Hubei Education Press, 2015).

Guo, Qinghua. "Yingzao Fashi: Twelfth-Century Chinese Building Manual," *Architectural History*, vol. 41 (1998): 1–13.

———. *The mingqi Pottery Buildings of Han Dynasty China 206 BC–AD 220: Architectural Representation and Represented Architecture* (Brighton England; Portland, OR: Sussex Academic Press, 2010).

Hainei shizhou ji 海内十洲记 [*Record of Ten Continents within the Seas*], in *Bowu zhi (wai qi zhong)* 博物志 (外七种), 101–112.

Han Baode 汉宝德, *Ming-Qing Jianzhu er'lun /Dougong de qiyuan yu fazhan* 明清建筑二论/斗栱的起源与发展 [*Theory on Architecture of the Ming-Qing Dynasties/The Origin and Development of Dougong*] (Beijing: Sanlian shudian, 2014).

Han Dian 汉典 [*Chinese Dictionary*], https://www.zdic.net/.

Han Yu 韩昱 and Guo Hongwu 郭洪武, "Confucianism in Caisson 藻井中的儒家文化," *Furniture Interior Design* 家具与室内装饰, no. 10 (2010): 40–41.

Harrer, Alexandra. *Fan-Shaped Bracket Sets and Their Application in Religious Timber Architecture of Shanxi Province* (University of Pennsylvania, 2010), PhD dissertation.

He Xiu 何休 [129–182] and Xu Yan 徐彦 [Tang], *Chunqiu Gongyang zhuan zhushu* 春秋公羊传注疏 (Shanghai: Shanghai guji chubanshe, 2014).

He Yan 何晏 [?–249], "*Jingfu dian fu* 景福殿赋 [*Rhapsody on the Hall of Great Blessings*]," in: *Zhaoming Wen Xuan*, 336–353. The English translation is by Knechtges in *Wen Xuan or Selections of Refined Literature, Volume II*, 279–304.

Hebei Provincial Museum 河北省博物馆, Taixi archeology brigade 文管处台西考古队, Theoretic team of Taixi brigade in Gaocheng county 河北省藁城县台西大队理论小组, *Gaocheng Taixi Shang dai yizhi* 藁城台西商代遗址 (Beijing: Wenwu chubanshe, 1977).

Henan Museum 河南博物院, ed., *Henan chutu Handai jianzhu mingqi* 河南出土汉代建筑明器 [*Han Dynasty Architectural Funerary Objects Unearthed in Henan*] (Zhengzhou: Daxiang chubanshe, 2002).

Henan Provincial Antiquities Institute 河南省文物考古研究所, ed., *Zhengzhou Shang cheng kaogu xin faxian yu yanjiu* 郑州商城考古新发与研究 1985–1992 [*New Archaeological Discoveries and Researches on the Shang City Site in Zhengzhou*] (Zhengzhou: Zhongzhou guji chubanshe, 1993).

Hou Fei 侯非, "The development of technological standardization in early China: the case study of the bronze fittings from the Spring and Autumn Period 从出土春秋铜构金缸看中国古代技术标准化发展," *Popular Standardization* 大众标准化, no. 11 (2014): 52–56.

Hu Dianyu 胡奠域 [Qing], *Qing Qianlong Ningyuan xian zhi xulue* 清乾隆宁远县志续略, ed., The Old Biographies Editorial Committee of Wushan county 武山县旧志整理编辑委员会 (Lanzhou: Gansu renmin chubanshe, 2005).

Hu, Jun. *Embracing the Circle: Domical Buildings in East Asian Architecture ca. 200–750* (Princeton University, 2014), PhD dissertation.

Huang Minglan 黄明兰 and Guo Yinqiang 郭引强, eds., *Luoyang Han mu bihua* 洛阳汉墓壁画 (Beijing: Wenwu chubanshe, 1996).

Institute of Cultural Relics Management of Santai County 三台县文物管理所, "Sichuan Santai Qijiang yamu qun 2000 niandu qingli jianbao 四川三台郪江崖墓群 2000 年度清理简报 [Report on the Clearing of Some Cliff Tombs on the Qi River at Santai, Sichuan]," *Kaogu* 考古 [*Archaeology*], no. 1 (2002), 16–41.

Jia Yi 贾谊 [200–168 BCE], *Xinshu* 新书 [*New Writings*] (Beijing: Zhonghua shuju, 2012).

Jiang Sheng 姜生, "Handai liexian tukao 汉代列仙图考 [A study of the portraits of immortals in the Han dynasty]," *Journal of Chinese Humanities* 文史哲, vol. 2 (2015): 17–33.

Jiao Xun 焦循 [1763–1820], *Qunjing gongshi tu* 群经宫室图 (printed in the Qing dynasty).

Kaogong ji 考工记 [Warring States], ed., Wen Renjun 闻人军 (Shanghai: Shanghai guji chubanshe, 2012).

Knapp, Ronald. *China's Old Dwellings* (Honolulu: University of Hawai'i Press, 2000).

Knechtges, David. trans. and annotator, *Wen Xuan or Selections of Refined Literature, Volume II: Rhapsodies on Sacrifices, Hunting, Travel, Sightseeing, Palaces and Halls, Rivers and Seas* (Princeton, NJ: Princeton University Press, 1983).

Lai, Delin. "Idealizing a Chinese style: rethinking early writings on Chinese architecture and the design of the National Central Museum in Nanjing," *Journal of the Society of Architectural Historians*, vol. 73, no. 1 (March 2014): 61–90.

Le Jiazao 乐嘉藻 [1867–1944], *Zhongguo jianzhu shi* 中国建筑史 [*History of Chinese Architecture*] (Nanchang: Jiangxi jiaoyu chubanshe, 2018).

Lewis, Mark Edward. *The Construction of Space in Early China* (Albany: State University of New York Press, 2006).

Leys, Simon. "The Chinese attitude towards the past," in: *The Hall of Uselessness: Collected Essays* (New York: New York Review Books, 2013), 285–301.

Li Caiqin 李采芹, *Zhongguo xiaofang wenshi zongtan* 中国消防文史丛谈 [*The Literature History of Fire Protection in China*] (Shanghai: Kexue jishu chubanshe, 2013).

Li Dou 李斗 [Qing], *Gongduan yingzao lu* 工段营造录 (Beijing: Architecture & Building Press, 2009).

Li Guoxin 李国新 and Yang Wenjing 杨蕴菁, eds., *Zhongguo Hanhua zaoxing yishu tudian-jianzhu* (ZHZYT-J) 中国汉画造型艺术图典-建筑 [*The Illustrated Compendium of Visual Arts in Chinese Han Reliefs: Architecture*] (Zhengzhou: Daxiang chubanshe, 2014).

Li Jie 李诫 [1035–1110], *Yingzao fashi* 营造法式 [*Building Standards*] (Beijing: Renmin chubanshe, 2011).

Li Qin 李琴, *Fu Hao xiaozun* 妇好鸮尊 [*Lady Hao's xiaozun*] (Zhengzhou: Daxiang chubanshe, 2017).

Li Shiqiao, "Reconstituting Chinese building tradition: the *Yingzao fashi* in the early twentieth century," *Journal of the Society of Architectural Historians*, vol. 62, no. 4 (2003): 470–489.

Li Yunhe 李允鉌, *Cathay's Idea: Design Theory of Chinese Classical Architecture* 华夏意匠: 中国古典建筑设计原理分析 (Tianjin: Tianjin University Press, 2013).

Liang Sicheng 梁思成 and Liu Zhiping 刘致平, "Dougong jianshuo 斗拱简说 [An introduction to bracket sets]," in: *Liang Sicheng quanji* 梁思成全集 [*The Complete Works of Liang Sicheng*] (Beijing: China Architecture & Building Press, 2001), VI, 291–324.

Liang Sicheng 梁思成, "Du Le Jiazao *Zhongguo jianhzu shi* pimiu 读乐嘉藻《中国建筑史》辟谬," in: Liang Sicheng, *Zhongguo jianhzu shi* 中国建筑史 [*History of Chinese Architecture*] (Tianjin: Baihua wenyi chubanshe, 1998), 361–370.

———, "Zaojing tianhua jianshuo 藻井天花简说 [Notes on ceilings]," in: *Liang Sicheng quanji* 梁思成全集 [*The Complete Works of Liang Sicheng*] (Beijing: China Architecture & Building Press, 2001), VI, 415–421.

———, ed., *Qing Gongbu gongcheng zuofa zeli tujie* 清工部工程做法则例图解 [*Illustrated Examples of the Engineering Methods of the Qing Ministry of Works*] (Beijing: Tsinghua University Press, 2006).

———, *Chinese Architecture: Art and Artifacts* 为什么研究中国建筑, ed., Lin Zhu 林洙 (Beijing: Foreign Language Teaching and Research Press, 2013).

Liji yizhu 礼记译注 [*The Annotation of Book of Rites*], ed., Yang Tianyu 杨天宇 (Shanghai: Shanghai guji chubanshe, 2016).

Liu An 刘安 [179–122 BCE] et al., *Huainan zi* 淮南子 [*Book of the King of Huainan*] (Beijing: Zhonghua shuju, 2014).

Liu Dunzhen 刘敦桢, *Zhongguo gudai jianzhu shi* 中国古代建筑史 [*History of Ancient Chinese Architecture*] (Beijing: China Architecture & Building Press, 1984).

———, *Liu Dunzhen wenji* (vol. 1) 刘敦桢文集（一）[*Collected Essays of Liu Dunzhen*] (Beijing: China Architecture & Building Press, 1982).

Liu Jie 刘杰, *Jiangnan mugou* 江南木构 [*Wood Construction South of the Yangtze*] (Shanghai: Shanghai Jiaotong University Press, 2009).

Liu Tianyang 刘天洋, "Shilun dougong chutiao de qiyuan yu zaoqi fazhan 试论斗拱出跳的起源与早期发展 [The origin of sticking out of dougong]," *Human Culture Heritage Preservation* 人类文化遗产保护, 2016(00): 115–121.

Liu Xiang 刘向 [77–6 BCE], *Lienü zhuan* 列女传 (Shenyang: Liaoning jiaoyu chubanshe, 1998).

Liu Xi 刘熙 [Han], *Shiming* 释名 [*Explaining Words*] (Beijing: Zhonghua shuju, 2016).

Liu Xujie 刘叙杰, "Handai dougong de leixing yu yanbian chutan 汉代斗拱的类型与演变初探 [A preliminary investigation of the types and evolution of Han bracket sets]," *Wenwu ziliao congkan* 文物资料丛刊 [*Cultural Relic Information Series*], 2 (1978): 222–228.

Lü Simian 吕思勉, "Pangu kao 盘古考 [Research on Pangu]," in: *Zhongguo shenhua xue bainian wenlun xuan* 中国神话学百年文论选 [*Collected Essays Celebrating the Centenary of Chinese Mythology Studies*], 2 vols (Xi'an: Shaanxi Normal University General Publishing House Co., Ltd., 2013), I, 252–255.

———, "Nüwa yu Gonggong 女娲与共工 [Nüwa and Gonggong]," in: *Zhongguo shenhua xue bainian wenlun xuan,* I, 246–251.

Lunyu 论语 [*Analects*] (Beijing: Renmin jiaoyu chubanshe, 2015).

Luo Zhewen 罗哲文, "Dougong 斗拱," *Wenwu cankao ziliao* 文物参考资料 [*Cultural Relics Reference Materials*], 1954(07): 44–61.

Miller, Tracy. *The Divine Nature of Power: Chinese Ritual Architecture at the Sacred Site of Jinci* (Cambridge, MA: Harvard University Press, 2007).

Ming'an 敏庵 [Qing], ed., *Baoguo si zhi* 保国寺志 [*History of Baoguo Temple*] (the collection of the temple, 1805).

Mote, F. W. "A millennium of Chinese urban history: form, time, and space concepts in Soochow," *The Rice University Studies*, vol. 59, no. 4 (1973): 35–65.

Murdoch, Iris. *The Sovereignty of Good* (London and New York: Routledge, 1970).

Nanjing Museum 南京博物院 and Cultural Relics Management Office of Shandong Province 山东省文物管理处, *Yi'nan guhuaxiang shimu fajue baogao* 沂南古画像石墓发掘报告 [*Report on the Excavation of a Tomb with Ancient Relief Sculptures in Yi'nan*] (Beijing: Cultural Relics Bureau under the Ministry of Culture, 1956).

Otto, Rudolf. *The Idea of the Holy: An Inquiry into the Non-Rational Factor in the Idea of the Divine and Its Relation to the Rational* (Beijing: China Social Sciences Publishing House, 1999).

Ouyang Xiu 欧阳修 [1007–1072] and Song Qi 宋祁 [998–1061], *Xin Tangshu* 新唐书 [*New History of the Tang*] (Beijing: Zhonghua shuju, 1975).

Pan Dehua 潘德华 and Pan Yexiang 潘叶祥, *Dougong* 斗拱 (Nanjing: Southeast University Press, 2011), 2 vols.

Pankenier, David. *Astrology and Cosmology in Early China: Conforming Earth to Heaven* (New York: Cambridge University Press, 2013).

Plato, *The Republic* (Minneapolis: Lerner Publishing Group, 1993).

Rao Zongyi 饶宗颐, "Hao Gong kao 蒿宫考 [Research on the Palace of Hao]," in: *Gu'an wenlu* 固庵文录 [*Collected Essays by Gu'an*] (Shenyang: Liaoning Education Press, 2000), 61–62.

Rong Geng 容庚 and Zhang Weichi 张维持, *Yin Zhou qingtong qi tonglun* 殷周青铜器通论 [*General Theory of the Shang-Zhou Bronzes*] (Beijing: Zhonghua shuju, 2012).

Ruan, Xing, *Confucius' Courtyard: Architecture, Philosophy and the Good Life in China* (London: Bloomsbury Visual Arts, 2022).

Rykwert, Joseph. *On Adam's House in Paradise: The Idea of the Primitive Hut in Architectural History* (Cambridge, MA: MIT Press, 1981).

Shandong Museum 山东博物馆, ed., *Yi'nan beizhai Hanmu huaxiang* 沂南北寨汉墓画像 [*Reliefs of the Beizhai Han Tomb in Yi'nan*] (Beijing: Wenwu chubanshe, 2015).

Shandong Museum 山东省博物馆, "Linbo Langjiazhuang yihao DongZhou xunren mu 临淄郎家庄一号东周殉人墓," *Kaogu xuebao* 考古学报, no. 1 (1977): 73–104.

Shanghai Museum 上海博物馆, *Shanghai bowuguan cang qingtong qi* 上海博物馆藏青铜器 [*Collections of the Bronzes in Shanghai Museum*] (Shanghai: Shanghai renmin meishu chubanshe, 1964).

Shang-Zhou Archaeology Team of the Department of History, Peking University 北京大学历史系考古教研室商周组, ed., *Shang Zhou kaogu* 商周考古 [*Archeology of the Shang-Zhou Dynasties*] (Beijing: Wenwu chubanshe, 1979).

Shanhai jing yizhu 山海经译注 [*The Annotated Classic of Mountains and Seas*] (Shanghai: Shanghai guji chubanshe, 2014).

Shanxi Provincial Cultural Relics Management Committee 山西省文物管理委会, "Shanxi Changzhishi Fenshuiling gumu de qingli 山西长治市分水岭古墓的清理 [The Clearing of an Ancient Tomb in Fengshuiling, Changzhi Municipality, Shanxi]," *Kaogu* 考古 [*Archaeology*], no. 1 (1957), 103–118.

Sima Qian 司马迁 [Western Han], *Shiji* 史记 [*The Grand Scribe's Records*] (Wuhan: Chongwen shuju, 2017), 4 vols.

———, "Tianguan shu 天官书 [Treatise on the Celestial Offices]," in: *Shiji* 史记 (Wuhan, 2017), vol. 1, 477–520.

Song Guoding 宋国定, "Bronze ornaments for buildings in the earlier Shang period and related problems 商代前期青铜建筑构件及相关问题," in: *Zhengzhou Shang cheng kaogu xin faxian yu yanjiu*, 72–77.

Song Yanping 宋艳萍, "Cong 'que' dao 'tianmen'—Han que de shenmihua licheng 从'阙'到'天门'—汉阙的神秘化历程 [From '*Que*' to the 'Gate of Heaven': the mystification process of the Han *Que*]," *Sichuan Cultural Relics* 四川文物, vol. 5 (2016): 60–68.

Soper, Alexander Coburn. "The 'Dome of Heaven' in Asia," *The Art Bulletin*, vol. 29, no. 4 (1947): 225–248.

Steinhardt, Nancy S. "Octagonal Halls and Octagonal Ceilings," *Proceedings from the Second International Conference on Chinese Architectural History*, Hangzhou, August 2001, 282–289.

———. *Chinese Architecture in an Age of Turmoil, 200–600* (Honolulu: University of Hawai'i Press, 2014).

Sun Xiaochun and Kistemaker, Jacob. *The Chinese Sky during the Han: Constellating Stars and Society* (Leiden: Brill, 1997).

Sun Zongwen 孙宗文, *Zhongguo jianzhu yu zhexue* 中国建筑与哲学 [*Chinese Architecture and Philosophy*] (Nanjing: Jiangsu kexue jishu chubanshe, 2000).

The Archaeological Team from Bureau of Culture in Henan Province 河南省文化局工作队, "Luoyang Xihan bihuamu fajue baogao 洛阳西汉壁画墓发掘报告 [Report on the Excavation of a Western Han Tomb with Wall Paintings at Luoyang]," *Kaogu xuebao* 考古学报 [*Acta Archeologica Sinica*], no. 2 (1964), 107–125.

The Editorial Committee of the complete murals in Dunhuang 中国敦煌壁画全集编辑委员会, ed., *Zhongguo Dunhuang bihua quanji* 中国敦煌壁画全集 (Tianjin: Renmin meishu chubanshe, 2002), vol. 1–11.

———, ed., *Zhongguo Dunhuang bihua quanji, Western Wei* 中国敦煌壁画全集 2 西魏 (Tianjin: Renmin meishu chubanshe, 2002), vol. 2.

The Institute of Archaeology CASS 中国社会科学院考古研究所, *Yinxu Fu Hao mu* 殷墟妇好墓 [*Lady Hao's Tomb at Yinxu*] (Beijing: Wenwu chubanshe, 1980).

The Institute of Archaeology, Chinese Academy of Sciences 中国科学院考古研究所, *Huixian fajue baogao* 辉县发掘报告 (Beijing: Kexue chubanshe, 1956).

The Institute of Archeology, Chinese Academy of Sciences 中国科学院考古研究所 and Shaanxi Xi'an Banpo Museum 陕西省西安半坡博物馆, *Xi'an Banpo* 西安半坡 (Beijing: Wenwu chubanshe, 1963).

Thompson, Lydia. *The Yi'nan Tomb: Narrative and Ritual in Pictorial Art of the Eastern Han (25–220 C.E.)* (New York University, 1998), PhD dissertation.

Thorp, Robert L. *China in the Early Bronze Age: Shang Civilization* (Philadelphia: University of Pennsylvania Press, 2006).

Tseng, Lillian Lan-ying. *Picturing Heaven in Early China* (Cambridge, MA; London: Harvard University Asia Center, 2011).

Tuan, Yi-Fu. *Dear Colleague: Common and Uncommon Observations* (Minneapolis: University of Minnesota Press, 2002).

———. *Humanist Geography: An Individual's Search for Meaning* (Staunton, VA: George F. Thompson Publishing, L.L.C., 2012).

———. *Passing Strange and Wonderful: Aesthetics, Nature, and Culture* (Washington, DC: Island Press, 1993).

———. *Space and Place: The Perspective of Experience* (Minneapolis: University of Minnesota Press, 2008).

Tuotuo 脱脱 [1314–1355], et al., *Songshi* 宋史 [*History of the Song Dynasty*] (Beijing: Zhonghua shuju, 1977).

Wang Jia 王嘉 [?–390], *Shiyi ji* 拾遗记 [*Record of Gleanings*], ed., Xiao Qi 萧绮 (Beijing: Zhonghua shuju, 1988).

Wang Pu 王溥 [922–982], *Tang huiyao* 唐会要 [*Institutional History of the Tang Dynasty*] (Beijing: Zhonghua shuju, 1955).

Wang Shilun 王士伦, ed., *Zhejiang chutu tongjing xuanji* 浙江出土铜镜选集 [*Collections of Bronze Mirrors Unearthed in Zhejiang*] (Beijing: Wenwu chubanshe, 2006).

Wang Yanshou 王延寿 [c.140–165], "Lu Lingguang dian fu 鲁灵光殿赋 [Rhapsody on the Hall of Numinous Brilliance in Lu]," in: *Zhaoming Wen Xuan* 昭明文选 [*Selections of Refined Literature*], ed., Xiao Tong 萧统 [501–531] (Beijing: Huaxia chubanshe, 2000), 324–335.

Wang, Aihe. *Cosmology and Political Culture in Early China* (Cambridge: Cambridge University Press, 2000).

Weber, Charles D. "Chinese pictorial bronze vessels of the late Chou period, Parts I," *Artibus Asiae*, vol. 28, no. 2/3 (1966): 107–154.

———. "Chinese pictorial bronze vessels of the late Chou period, Parts II," *Artibus Asiae*, vol. 28, no. 4 (1966): 271–311.

———. "Chinese pictorial bronze vessels of the late Chou period, Parts III," *Artibus Asiae*, vol. 29, no. 2/3 (1967): 115–192.

———. "Chinese pictorial bronze vessels of the late Chou period, Parts IV," *Artibus Asiae*, vol. 30, no. 2/3 (1968): 145–236.

Wei Qiuping 魏秋萍, "Supplementary textual research on 'Dongjing jiehuo' of pottery wells and reliefs '东井戒火' 陶井画像补证," *Wenbo* 文博, no. 04 (2013): 46–49.

Wheatley, Paul. *The Origins and Character of the Ancient Chinese City*, 2 vols (Somerset, NJ: Aldine Transaction, 2008).

Wright, Arthur F. "The cosmology of the Chinese city," in: *The City in Late Imperial China*, ed., G. W. Skinner (Taipei: SMC Publishing Inc., 1997), 33–37.

Wu Hung. *Monumentality in Early Chinese Art and Architecture* (Stanford: Stanford University Press, 1995).

———. *The Art of the Yellow Springs: Understanding Chinese Tombs* (London: Reaktion Books, 2010).

———. *The Wu Liang Shrine: The Ideology of Early Chinese Pictorial Art* (Stanford: Stanford University Press, 1989).

———. "Xiwangmu, the Queen Mother of the West," *Orientations*, vol. 18, no. 4 (April 1987): 24–33.

Wu Qingzhou 吴庆洲, *Jianzhu zheli, yijiang yu wenhua* 建筑哲理, 意匠与文化 [*Architectural Philosophy, Artistic Conception and Culture*] (Beijing: China Architecture & Building Press, 2005).

Xiao Mo 萧默, *Dunhuang jianzhu yanjiu* 敦煌建筑研究 [*Research on the Architecture of Dunhuang*] (Beijing: China Architecture & Building Press, 2019).

Xie Qinguo 谢清果 and Zhang Dan 张丹, "Guanxiang zhiqi; Xia Shang shiqi qingtongqi tuxiang de wenhua fuhao biaozheng 观象制器：夏商周时期青铜器图像的文化符号表征 [Inventing Wares and Utensils by Observing the Images: Representation of Bronze Images as Cultural Symbols in Xia, Shang and Zhou Dynasties]," *Signs & Media* 符号与传媒, 2018(02): 77–92.

Xie, Jing and Heath, Tim. *Heritage-Led Urban Regeneration in China* (New York and London: Routledge, 2017).

Xie, Jing. "Transcending the Limitations of Physical Form: A Case Study of Cang Lang Pavilion," *Journal of Architecture*, vol. 21, no. 5 (2016): 691–718.

———. "From earth to heaven: the origin and development of zaojing in early China," *arq: Architectural Research Quarterly*, vol. 23, no. 4 (2019): 349–363.

———. "Pillar of Heaven: the symbolic function of column-and-bracket sets in the Han dynasty," *Architectural History*, vol. 63 (2020): 1–36.

Xijing zaji (wai wu zhong) 西京杂记 (外五种) [*Miscellanea of the Western Capital (And Five Other Essays)*], ed., Wang Genlin 王根林 (Shanghai: Shanghai guji chubanshe, 2012).

Xiong Long 熊龙, "Textual research on the wordings 'Dongjing jiehuo' of pottery wells '东井戒火' 陶井正名及相关问题考证," *Wenbo* 文博, no. 01 (2012): 38–44.

Xu Shen 许慎 [Han], *Shuowen jiezi zhu* 说文解字注 [*Explaining Depictions of Reality and Analyzing Graphs of Words*], ed., Duan Yucai 段玉裁 [Qing] (Shanghai: Shanghai guji chubanshe, 2019).

Yan Dan zi 燕丹子 [Prince Dan of Yan], in *Bowu zhi* (*wai qi zhong*) 博物志 (外七种), 69–84.

Yang Hongxun 杨鸿勋, "Dougong qiyuan kaocha斗拱起源考察 [Research of the origin of Dougong]," in: Yang Hongxun, *Jianzhu kaoguxue lunwenji*, 253–267.

———, "Hemudu yizhi mugou shuijing jianding 河姆渡遗址木构水井鉴定[Appraisal of the wooden water well in Hemudu relic]," in: Yang Hongxun, *Jianzhu kaoguxue lunwenji*, 52–57.

———, "Fengxiang chutu Chunqiu Qin gong tonggou-jingang 凤翔出土春秋秦宫铜构—金釭 [The bronze fittings of the Qin palace during the Spring and Autumn Period unearthed from the Fengxiang site]," *Kaogu* 考古, 1976 (02): 103–108.

———, *Jianzhu kaoguxue lunwenji* 建筑考古学论文集 [*Collected Essays on Architecture Archaeology*] (Beijing: Wenwu chubanshe, 1987).

Yang Jie 杨洁, "Cuo jinyin silong sifeng tongfangan jianshang 错金银四龙四凤铜方案鉴赏 [The appraisal of the bronze square stable with gold and silver inlay and four dragons and four phoenixes]," *World of Antiquity* 文物世界, no. 6 (2014): 72–74.

Yi Hongbing 尹弘兵, "Zhou Zhaowang nanzheng duixiang kao 周昭王南征对象考 [Research on the Zhou Zhaowang's south conquests]," *Renwen zazhi* 人文杂志, 2008(02): 159–163.

Yin Weizhang 殷玮璋, "Excavation report of the Eastern Zhou copper mining relic in Tonglü Mountain Hubei 湖北铜绿山东周铜矿遗址发掘," *kaogu* 考古, no. 1 (1981): 19–23.

Ying Shao 应劭 [Eastern Han], *Fengsu tongyi jiaozhu* 风俗通义校注 [*Comprehensive Meanings of Popular Customs*] (Beijing: Zhonghua shuju, 2015).

Yu Zhuoyun 于倬云, "Dougong de yunyong shi woguo gudai jianzhu jishu de zhongyao gongxian 斗拱的运用是我国古代建筑技术的重要贡献 [The important contribution of bracketing to our country's ancient architectural technology]," in: *Zhongguo gongdian jianzhu lunwen ji* 中国宫殿建筑论文集 [*Collected Essays on Palace Architecture in China*] (Beijing: Zijincheng chubanshe, 2002), 165–193.

Zhang Changshou 张长寿, *Shang Zhou kaogu lunji* 商周考古论集 [*Collected Essays of the Shang-Zhou Archaeology*] (Beijing: Wenwu chubanshe, 2007).

Zhang Heng 张衡 [79–139], "*Xijing fu* 西京赋," in: *Zhaoming Wen Xuan*, 37–67. The English translation by Knechtges, *Wen Xuan or Selections of Refined Literature, Volume I*, 181–242.

Zhang Junru 张俊儒, "Shoumianwen qingtong jianzhu goujian 兽面纹青铜建筑构件," online: http://www.chnmus.net/sitesources/hnsbwy/page_pc/dzjp/mzyp/smwqtjzgj/list1.html <accessed 22 June 2019>.

Zhang Shuxian 张淑娴, "The transformation and cultural meanings of zaojing in ancient Chinese architecture 中国古代建筑藻井装饰的演变及其文化内涵," *World of Antiquity* 文物世界, no. 6 (2003): 35–41.

Zhang Tingyu 张廷玉 [1672–1755], *Mingshi* 明史 [*History of the Ming Dynasty*], 6 vols (Beijing: Guojia tushuguan chubanshe, 2014).

Zhang Xin 张辛, "qingtong qi liyi lunyao 青铜器礼义论要 [Discussion on the etiquette and meanings of bronze vessels]," *Kaogu yanjiu* 考古研究, 2006 (00): 572–586.

Zhang Yijie 张毅捷, Li Yin 李寅, and Han Xiao 韩效 "The origin of the pu-pai-fang (plate) 试论普拍方的起源," *Huazhong Architecture* 华中建筑, no. 5 (2018), 118–120.

Zhejiang Culture Relics Management Committee 浙江省文物管理委员会 and Zhejiang Provincial Museum 浙江省博物馆, "Hemudu yizhi diyiqi fajue baogao 河姆渡遗址第一期发掘报告 [The phase one excavation report of Hemudu relic]," *Kaogu Xuebao* 考古学报, no. 1 (1978): 39–94.

Zheng Jiexiang 郑杰祥, "The discussion of the function of the bronze architectural fitting from the Xiaoshuangqiao site 关于小双桥遗址出土青铜建筑饰器功用的探讨," *Gudai wenming yanjiu tongxun* 古代文明研究通讯, 2008(38): 28–31.

Zheng Qiao 郑樵 [1104–1162], *Tongzhi lue* 通志略 (Shanghai: Shanghai guji chubanshe, 1990).

Zhong Xiaoqing 钟晓青, "Dougong, puzuo, yu puzuo ceng 斗拱, 铺作, 与铺作层 [Dougong, puzuo, and puzuo layers]," *Zhongguo jianzhu shilun huikan* 中国建筑史论汇刊, no. 1 (2008): 3–26.

Zhong Zhi 钟治, "Clearing-up of some cliff tombs on the Qi River at Santai, Sichuan 四川三台郪江崖墓群 2000 年度清理简报," *kaogu* 考古, no. 1 (2002): 16–41.

Zhu Fenghan 朱凤瀚, *Gudai Zhongguo qingtong qi* 古代中国青铜器 [*Ancient Chinese Bronzes*] (Tianjin: Nankai University Press, 1995).

Zhu Xilu 朱锡禄, ed., *Wushi ci Han huaxiang shi* 武氏祠汉画像石 [*Han Relief Sculptures in the Wu Family Shrine*] (Jinan: Shandong meishu chubanshe, 1986).

Zou Houben 邹厚本, "Chunqiu shengyu zhuangshi goujian 春秋乘舆装饰构件 [The ornament fitting for carriage from the Spring and Autumn Period]," in: *The Collection Category of Nanjing Museum* 南京博物院藏宝录 (Shanghai: Wenyi chubanshe; Sanlian shudian, 1992), 162–163.

Zuo Qiouming 左丘明 [502–422 BCE], *Zuozhuan zhushu* 左傳注疏 [*Annotations of the Commentary of Zuo*], eds., Tu Yu 杜預 [Jin] and 孔颖达 Kong Yingda [Tang] (copyediting by Ruan Yuan in the Qing dynasty), ch. 21, pp. 433–434, online: http://tk.cepiec.com.cn <accessed 20 February 2020>.

INDEX

CPSIA information can be obtained
at www.ICGtesting.com
Printed in the USA
JSHW030939210323
39224JS00001B/1

9 781785 279423